HEALTHY HEART

First published in Great Britain by Simon & Schuster UK Ltd, 2005
A Viacom Company

Simon & Schuster UK Ltd
Africa House
64–78 Kingsway
London
WC2B 6AH

1 3 5 7 9 10 8 6 4 2

Design: **Fiona Andreanelli**
Food photography: **Juliet Piddington**
Home economist: **Kim Morphew**
Stylist for food photography: **Helen Trent**
Copy-editor: **Nicole Foster**
Proofreader: **Michèle Clarke**
Indexer: **Deborah Savage**
Printed and bound in China

ISBN 0 74325 978 5

Best-kept Secrets of the Women's Institute

HEALTHY HEART

Elspeth Smith

SIMON & SCHUSTER
A VIACOM COMPANY

ACKNOWLEDGEMENTS

My thanks to WI Enterprises for inviting me to compile this book and allowing a long-held ambition to be fulfilled.

Equally, thanks to Andy, Graham and Kathryn who have been willing and honest tasters of my recipes over the years and, most recently, managed to survive 'computer deprivation' while I commandeered the keyboard for hours on end writing up the manuscript.

Finally, appreciation to my mother May Thomson who, during my early years, encouraged and developed my cooking skills and interest in good, home-prepared food.

CONTENTS

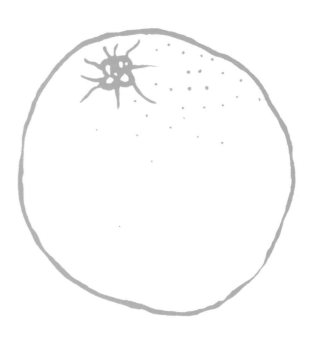

'You are what you eat' is certainly true in the case of heart health, but eating healthily need not be boring. In fact, the opposite is true – by eating as wide and varied a diet as possible you will ensure that you get all the different nutrients your body needs as well as helping to protect your heart.

Many of us don't think too deeply about healthy eating until a doctor tells us otherwise. This was certainly the case in our family until a number of years ago when my mother developed severe angina and subsequently had to undergo by-pass surgery. As a family, we could not have been accused of eating unhealthily or excessively, it was simply that she was one of those people whose body made too

INTRODUCTION

much cholesterol and over the years her arteries had become blocked. It turned out that she has familial hypercholesterolaemia and so my brother and I are also at risk. The good thing is that it has allowed us the opportunity to assess and improve our diet and lifestyle so that we can take steps to greatly reduce a number of the factors that can cause cardiovascular disease.

Over the years we have revised what we consumed in order to eat as wide a range of nutritious foods as possible, taking them from all the major food groups. Of course, there are some foods that should be eaten less frequently than others, but it is better to think of it in terms of moderation rather than being deprived. So what are the guidelines to follow to reduce the risks?

FRUIT & VEGETABLES

An amazing amount of information has been discovered about how eating fruit and vegetables improves our health, and they definitely play a huge part in looking after the heart and cardiovascular system. Fruit and vegetables contain high levels of the antioxidants vitamins C and E and beta-carotene, and phyto-chemicals such as flavenoids which inhibit the damaging action of free radicals in the body. By preventing oxidation, this reduces the amount of cholesterol forming in the blood and the subsequent narrowing of the arteries with fatty deposits.

The mineral potassium is also found in good quantities in fruit and vegetables and it plays an important role in helping to control blood pressure. Equally, recent research has found a strong link between raised levels of homocysteine in the blood and incidence of heart disease, but B vitamins, and in particular B6 (folic acid), may help to reverse this situation. The B group of vitamins is found in green vegetables and pulses. Soluble fibre from citrus fruits and apples, oats and pulses also helps to reduce blood cholesterol levels.

You can see how vital a sufficient intake of fruit and vegetables is to our heart health. We should all try to eat at least five portions of fruit and vegetables a day and take this as a minimum amount. So over the years I have tried to incorporate lots more fruit and vegetables into the recipes for our meals so that we are consuming what we need without even really having to think about it. If we are able to build on that and eat even more, it can only be to our benefit in many different ways.

FATS & OILS

The initial reaction when considering how to eat for a healthy heart is to reduce fat to an absolute minimum or even do without. However, although too much is not a good idea, it is vital to have a small amount of fat in our diet. What we should try to do is eat the right type of fat rather than cutting out fat completely. We need to greatly reduce the saturated fat we consume because it tends to raise blood cholesterol levels. Saturated fat is mostly found in animal products, such as butter, cream, cheese and the fat on meat, and processed foods like cakes, biscuits, pastries and snack foods. Also take care to avoid trans-fatty acids, which again raise cholesterol levels. They are likely to be found in processed foods, hard margarines and dairy products.

Instead, we should be eating the unsaturated fats. Look out for polyunsaturated fats found in nuts, seeds and grains such as sunflower, soya and corn. A particularly good type of polyunsaturated fat, known as omega-3 fatty acids, comes from oily fish such as tuna, trout, mackerel, sardines and salmon, and it helps to reduce the tendency of the blood to clot. We should try to have a serving of one of these fish at least once a week.

As well as the polyunsaturated fats, we should be incorporating mono-unsaturated fats into our diet. These mostly come from olive and rapeseed oils, nuts and avocados. It is thought that mono-unsaturated fats lower the 'bad' LDL cholesterol and increase slightly the levels of 'good' HDL cholesterol.

SALT

I have found that it takes only a few simple changes to reduce a lot of the saturated fat from our meals. Here are a few suggestions:

- **replace high fat dairy products with lower fat alternatives – most cheeses, yogurts, creams, etc. can now be found in reduced fat varieties without the flavour being compromised**

- **replace butter with an unsaturated fat spread**

- **always measure the amount of oil being added to a pan rather than just 'glugging' it in, as is so popular with TV chefs!**

- **buy low fat salad dressings and mayonnaise, or make your own using polyunsaturated fats, such as sunflower oil, or olive oil which contains mono-unsaturated fats**

- **avoid fried take-away foods and commercially produced cakes and biscuits**

- **always buy meat as lean as possible and trim off any visible fat**

- **remove the skin from chicken and turkey portions**

- **use non-stick pans for cooking so that the tiniest amount of oil (or none at all) can be used for sautéing, and line cake tins with non-stick baking parchment instead of greasing liberally.**

Unfortunately, most of us eat far more salt than we actually need, and the problem is that a high intake of salt is linked with raised blood pressure and heart disease. We can, with a little thought, reduce the amount of salt we consume and retrain our taste buds to do without. I now use very little salt in cooking (most of the recipes in the book only mention salt where it seems to be essential). Make good use of flavourings such as freshly ground black pepper, herbs, spices and lemon juice and really enjoy the natural flavour of food.

Cutting out processed foods as much as possible and not sprinkling salt on food at the table will go a long way to reduce salt intake. Look out for low salt varieties of items such as bacon, baked beans, soy sauce, etc. when shopping.

I hope you will see that my aim in compiling the recipes for this book has been to share my discovery that eating for a healthy heart does not have to be boring or lacking in flavour. I have tried to keep saturated fat and salt to a minimum, while making the most of the wonderful range of fruit and vegetables available to us now. The dishes are tasty, nutritious and easy to prepare, with the whole family in mind. It is never too early to start taking care of your heart and I'm sure you will find that food that is good for you, actually tastes good as well.

Many of our traditional and well-loved starters and soups are high in fat and calories, while snacks and light meals can be an absolute minefield, highly dependent on cheese, chips or pastry!

Yet soups can be a wonderful choice, both for starting a meal and also for a light lunch. They allow you to incorporate lots of healthy vegetables and, in the case of the recipes in this chapter, are also fairly low in fat. Go for the wonderful Mediterranean flavours of the Italian Bean Soup or the warmth of the Seriously

SOUPS, STARTERS & SNACKS

Spicy Lentil Soup and simply accompany them with some crusty bread. On the other hand, the Pea & Mint Soup and the Red Pepper, Sweet Potato & Vine Tomato Soup are elegant enough for a dinner party.

The other starters can double up as a quick meal or a snack – a little of the Smoked Mackerel & Rocket Pâté spread on a couple of oat cakes is brilliant as a 'munchie preventer' when you hit that hunger hole in the middle of the afternoon! Or why not keep some of the Chunky Spiced Houmous in the fridge with a little pot of crudités on stand-by, for a snack attack?

A wonderfully robust soup **based on the traditional Indian dhal**, with the lentils providing useful amounts of soluble fibre. The quantity of chilli powder in the recipe gives a medium spiciness and heat, but adjust it according to your own taste.

SERIOUSLY SPICY LENTIL SOUP

1 tablespoon vegetable oil
1 onion, chopped
1 red pepper, de-seeded and diced
2 garlic cloves, crushed
2.5 cm (1 inch) piece fresh root ginger, peeled and chopped finely
$^1/_2$ teaspoon chilli powder
$^1/_2$ teaspoon turmeric powder
$^1/_2$ teaspoon ground coriander
225 g (8 oz) split red lentils
850 ml (1$^1/_2$ pints) vegetable stock
400 g tin of chopped tomatoes
1 tablespoon tomato purée
freshly ground black pepper

TO GARNISH:
low fat plain yogurt
fresh coriander leaves

1   Heat the vegetable oil in a large saucepan and gently fry the chopped onion for 3–4 minutes until softened but not coloured. Stir in the diced red pepper and crushed garlic and cook for a further 3–4 minutes.

2   Add the ginger, chilli powder, turmeric, ground coriander and lentils. Stir well to coat with the oil. Add the vegetable stock, chopped tomatoes and tomato purée, stir and bring up to the boil. Reduce the heat, cover the pan and simmer the soup for 20–25 minutes, stirring occasionally, until the lentils are cooked.

3   Liquidise or process half the soup to give a chunky texture. If you prefer a smoother textured soup, then purée the whole amount. Reheat the soup, adjusting the seasoning to taste. Ladle into warmed bowls and garnish with a swirl of yogurt and some fresh coriander leaves.

SERVES 6
PREPARATION & COOKING TIME:
20 minutes + 40 minutes cooking
FREEZING: not recommended

PER SERVING: 207 calories, 8 g fat

There's a real **flavour of the Mediterranean** in this filling soup. Using canned beans makes the preparation so much speedier than with dried beans, which have to be soaked beforehand. However, do remember to rinse the canned beans thoroughly to wash off any excess saltiness from the brine. Serve this recipe as a 'main course' soup accompanied by sunblush tomato and olive bread (page 76).

ITALIAN BEAN SOUP

2 tablespoons olive oil
50 g (1³/₄ oz) cubetti di pancetta
1 onion, chopped
1 celery stick, trimmed and diced
1 carrot, diced
1 garlic clove, crushed
¹/₂ teaspoon dried sage
1 bay leaf
400 g can of chopped tomatoes
1 litre (1³/₄ pints) vegetable stock
400 g can of borlotti beans,
rinsed and drained
400 g can of cannellini beans,
rinsed and drained
100 g (3¹/₂ oz) French beans,
cut into 4 cm (1¹/₂ inch) lengths
75 g (2³/₄ oz) spaghetti,
broken into short pieces
1 tablespoon chopped fresh flat leaf parsley
freshly ground black pepper

1 Heat the olive oil in a large saucepan. Add the pancetta and fry gently for 2–3 minutes. Stir in the onion, celery, carrot, garlic, sage and bay leaf. Cook gently for a further 4–5 minutes to soften the vegetables.

2 Stir in the chopped tomatoes and vegetable stock. Bring up to the boil then reduce the heat, cover the pan and simmer gently for 15 minutes. Add the borlotti and cannellini beans and simmer for a further 5 minutes. Remove the bay leaf.

3 Ladle half the soup into a liquidiser or food processor and blend until smooth. Return the purée to the pan with the French beans and spaghetti pieces. Cook for 7–8 minutes until the spaghetti is 'al dente' and the French beans just tender.

4 Remove from the heat and stir in the chopped parsley. Check the seasoning and add some freshly ground black pepper if required. Serve immediately in warmed bowls.

SERVES 4
PREPARATION TIME: 15 minutes + 1 hour chilling
FREEZING: not recommended

SMOKED MACKEREL & ROCKET PÂTÉ

This pâté is delicious as a starter or a light lunch. Serve with slices of wholemeal toast or warm wholemeal rolls and a salad garnish. The **warm peppery flavour** of rocket leaves complements the richness of the smoked mackerel perfectly.

PER SERVING: 217 calories, 14 g fat

50 g pack of rocket leaves
225 g (8 oz) smoked mackerel fillets, skinned and flaked
250 g tub of Quark
1 teaspoon horseradish sauce
a squeeze of fresh lemon juice
freshly ground black pepper

1   Place the rocket leaves, smoked mackerel, Quark and horseradish sauce into a food processor. Give several pulses to purée the ingredients, scraping round the sides of the bowl in between, to create a textured pâté.
2   Check the seasoning and add a generous squeeze of lemon juice and some freshly ground black pepper to taste.
3   Transfer to four individual ramekin dishes or one larger bowl, cover and chill for about 1 hour before serving.

SERVES 4–6
PREPARATION & COOKING TIME: 30 minutes
FREEZING: not recommended

SWEET RED PEPPER & COURGETTE FRITTATA

Full of flavoursome vegetables, this frittata makes a light meal served with a crisp green salad. Otherwise, allow it to cool, chill it and cut into wedges to make an **excellent addition to a picnic** for outdoor eating, or to a lunchbox as a change from sandwiches.

PER SERVING: 137 calories, 9 g fat

1 tablespoon olive oil
4 small new potatoes, unpeeled and cut into 1 cm ($\frac{1}{2}$ inch) dice
1 small red onion, sliced
1 garlic clove, chopped finely
1 red pepper, de-seeded and sliced
1 small courgette, cut into 5 mm ($\frac{1}{4}$ inch) slices
6 eggs, lightly beaten
150 g (5$\frac{1}{2}$ oz) baby plum tomatoes, halved
freshly ground black pepper

1   Heat the oil in a large frying pan, at least 25 cm (10 inches) in diameter, and add the cubed potatoes, red onion and garlic. Cook over a medium heat for about 10 minutes until the potatoes are just tender. Stir frequently to prevent the vegetables browning. Add the pepper and courgette and cook for another 5 minutes.
2   Pour the beaten egg into the pan and scatter in the tomatoes. Allow to cook gently for about 5 minutes, without stirring, until the egg is beginning to set.
3   Transfer the pan and place it underneath a medium hot grill for 2–3 minutes (taking care that the pan handle is away from the heat) until the frittata is completely set and lightly golden. Remove from the heat, allow to rest for a couple of minutes and then slide the frittata on to a warmed plate and cut it into four or six wedges for serving.

RED PEPPER, SWEET POTATO & VINE TOMATO SOUP

The hint of chilli powder and cumin makes this a **warming** soup for the cooler days of autumn and winter. Using vine tomatoes, although slightly more expensive, really enhances the flavour of the soup.

PER SERVING: 99 calories, 3 g fat

1 tablespoon olive oil
1 onion, chopped
2 garlic cloves, crushed
2 red peppers, de-seeded and cubed
250 g (9 oz) sweet potato, peeled and cubed
350 g (12 oz) vine tomatoes, de-seeded and chopped roughly
a pinch of chilli powder
½ teaspoon ground cumin
850 ml (1½ pints) vegetable stock
½ teaspoon sugar
freshly ground black pepper

TO GARNISH:
low fat plain yogurt
chopped fresh parsley

1　Heat the olive oil in a large saucepan and gently cook the onion and garlic for 5 minutes until softened but not browned. Stir in the red peppers, sweet potato and vine tomatoes along with the chilli powder and ground cumin. Cook for a further 5 minutes to soften the vegetables.

2　Pour in the stock, bring up to the boil, reduce the heat and then cover and leave to simmer for 20 minutes until the vegetables are tender.

3　Using a liquidiser or food processor, purée the soup in batches. Pass the soup through a sieve to remove any small pieces of tomato skin and return it to the rinsed-out saucepan. Stir in the sugar and check the seasoning, adding some freshly ground black pepper, if desired. Gently reheat the soup, then serve immediately in warmed bowls, garnishing with a swirl of yogurt and a sprinkling of chopped parsley.

SERVES 4
PREPARATION & COOKING TIME:
15 minutes + 45 minutes cooking
FREEZING: not recommended

GOLDEN BROTH

A traditional soup **from Northern Ireland** thickened with oatmeal and full of delicious vegetables – ideal for providing the soluble fibre and antioxidants to ward off heart disease. Don't worry if it looks as if you have too much spinach to fit into the pan, it wilts down very quickly as soon as it touches the liquid. To make a healthy lunch, serve the soup with some warm, freshly baked wholemeal soda bread.

PER SERVING: 160 calories, 8 g fat

25 g (1 oz) **sunflower margarine**
1 large **onion, chopped finely**
1 **celery stick, peeled and chopped finely**
2 **carrots, quartered lengthways and chopped finely**
25 g (1 oz) **plain flour**
600 ml (1 pint) **chicken stock**
300 ml (½ pint) **semi skimmed milk**
25 g (1 oz) **medium oatmeal**
125 g (4½ oz) **spinach, chopped roughly**
freshly ground black pepper

1 Melt the sunflower margarine in a large saucepan. Add the onion, celery and carrots and cook for 4–5 minutes to just soften the vegetables.
2 Stir in the flour and cook for a further minute, stirring constantly. Pour in the chicken stock followed by the milk and bring to the boil, stirring, to thicken the soup slightly. Reduce the heat, cover the pan and simmer gently for 30 minutes. Stir occasionally.
3 Sprinkle the oatmeal over the surface of the soup and stir it in. Add the chopped spinach and stir that in. Continue to cook gently for a further 10–15 minutes, stirring occasionally to prevent the soup sticking.
4 Check the seasoning and adjust to taste, then serve the soup immediately in warmed bowls.

SERVES 4
PREPARATION & COOKING TIME:
15 minutes + 30 minutes cooking
FREEZING: not recommended

PEA & MINT SOUP

This soup has a wonderful fresh flavour and colour that speak of spring and summer even though it uses frozen peas. Since they are harvested and frozen so quickly, frozen peas often contain higher amounts of vitamin C than if the peas had been sitting on a greengrocer's shelf for a while. Of course, if you have peas and mint fresh from the garden, that's even better. Using half fat crème fraîche instead of double cream is much healthier but still provides the smoothness called for in a creamed soup.

PER SERVING: 206 calories, 9 g fat

1 bunch of **spring onions, trimmed and chopped**
1 **potato, peeled and cubed**
2 tablespoons **chopped fresh mint plus a few sprigs**
850 ml (1½ pints) **vegetable stock**
500 g (1 lb 2 oz) **frozen garden peas**
200 ml (7 fl oz) **half fat crème fraîche**
freshly ground black pepper

1 Place the spring onions, cubed potato and three sprigs of fresh mint in a large saucepan. Pour over the vegetable stock and bring up to the boil. Reduce the heat, cover and simmer gently for 15 minutes until the potato cubes are tender.
2 Add the peas, bring back to simmering point and cook for a further 5 minutes until the peas are tender. Remove the pan from the heat and discard the sprigs of mint.
3 Pour the soup into a food processor or blender and process until smooth. This may need to be done in two or three batches.
4 Return the soup to the pan and stir in the crème fraîche and the chopped mint. Reheat the soup gently, but do not allow to boil. Check the seasoning and add a little freshly ground black pepper if required. Serve the soup in warmed bowls and garnish each with a small sprig of fresh mint.

SERVES 4
PREPARATION & COOKING TIME:
25 minutes + 25 minutes cooking
FREEZING: not recommended

PER SERVING: 170 calories, 10 g fat

1 tablespoon extra virgin olive oil plus extra
for greasing
4 large field or portobello mushrooms
1 egg, lightly beaten
2 garlic cloves, chopped finely
1 small tomato, de-seeded
and chopped finely
75 g (2³/₄ oz) fresh wholemeal breadcrumbs
125 g ball light mozzarella cheese,
cubed finely
1 tablespoon snipped fresh chives
1 tablespoon chopped fresh flat leaf parsley
freshly ground black pepper
2 tablespoons freshly grated
Parmesan cheese

This is one of my favourite ways of serving **large field or portobello mushrooms**. It makes an excellent starter for four people with a light salad garnish or makes an equally tasty 'veggie' main course for two. Use wholemeal breadcrumbs for preference since they add a lovely depth of flavour.

1. Preheat the oven to Gas Mark 6/electric oven 200°C/fan oven 180°C.
2. Lightly oil a shallow ovenproof dish large enough to contain the four mushrooms in a single layer.
3. Detach the stalks from the mushrooms and chop these stalks finely.
4. Place the beaten egg in a medium bowl and add the chopped mushroom stalks, garlic and tomato, 50 g (1³/₄ oz) breadcrumbs, the cubed mozzarella, chives and parsley. Season with a grinding of black pepper.
5. Mix everything well together to form a stuffing and use it to fill the mushroom caps. Place the filled mushrooms in the baking dish.
6. Sprinkle the mushrooms with remaining breadcrumbs.
7. Bake in the oven for 20–25 minutes until the breadcrumb topping is crisp and golden brown and the mushrooms are tender. Serve immediately with Parmesan cheese.

GARLICKY STUFFED MUSHROOMS

SERVES 6
PREPARATION & COOKING TIME: 25 minutes
FREEZING: not recommended

CHUNKY SPICED HOUMOUS

With its spices and added vegetables, this recipe gives houmous a bit more interest than the usual shop-bought variety. It is also **wonderfully versatile** – serve it as a starter on individual plates with a salad garnish and fingers of Melba toast, or use it to fill warmed pitta breads along with sliced tomatoes and cucumber for a speedy snack, or it could even be part of a buffet selection with colourful crudités for dipping. It will keep happily in the fridge in a covered container for several days.

PER SERVING: 194 calories, 13 g fat

2 x 400 g cans of chick peas, rinsed and drained
4 tablespoons extra virgin olive oil
juice of 1 small lemon
1 red onion, chopped
1 garlic clove, chopped finely
1 teaspoon ground cumin
$\frac{1}{2}$ teaspoon ground coriander
$\frac{1}{4}$ teaspoon chilli powder
2 tomatoes, de-seeded and chopped finely
1 tablespoon chopped fresh coriander
salt and freshly ground black pepper

1   Put the chick peas in a food processor with 3 tablespoons of olive oil and the lemon juice. Blend to a rough purée. Transfer to a bowl.
2   Heat the remaining tablespoon of oil in a frying pan and gently cook the onion for 5–6 minutes. Add the chopped garlic and continue to cook for a further 4–5 minutes until softened. Remove from the heat and allow to cool.
3   Add the onion and garlic to the puréed chick peas together with the spices, tomatoes and chopped coriander. Carefully stir to combine all the ingredients, then season to taste with salt and black pepper. Serve as suggested above.

SERVES 4
PREPARATION & COOKING TIME: 35 minutes
FREEZING: not recommended

WARM CHICKEN & MUSHROOM SALAD

A quick to prepare, light meal **for serving on those chillier days** during the summer when something warm is called for. Equally, it could be served in smaller portions and used as a starter for six people.

PER SERVING: 467 calories, 19 g fat

3 tablespoons extra virgin olive oil
1 red onion, sliced
1 garlic clove, chopped finely
150 g (5$\frac{1}{2}$ oz) chestnut mushrooms, quartered
4 skinless, boneless chicken breasts, cubed
2 tablespoons clear honey
1 tablespoon coarse-grain mustard
2 tablespoons white wine vinegar
freshly ground black pepper
1 large bag of ready prepared mixed salad leaves
$\frac{1}{2}$ cucumber, diced
100 g (3$\frac{1}{2}$ oz) cherry tomatoes, halved

1   Heat 1 tablespoon of the olive oil in a large pan and cook the sliced onion and garlic for 4–5 minutes until softened. Add the mushrooms to the pan and cook for a further 3–4 minutes. Remove the onions and mushrooms from the pan and set aside.
2   Add the remaining 2 tablespoons of oil to the pan and fry the cubes of chicken over a moderate heat until they are golden brown and cooked through. Add the honey, mustard and white wine vinegar, mixing well to coat the chicken with the dressing. Return the onion and mushrooms to the pan and cook for a further minute to warm through. Season with freshly ground black pepper.
3   Divide the salad leaves between four plates and scatter over the diced cucumber and cherry tomatoes. Top with the cooked chicken mixture and drizzle over any remaining warm dressing from the pan. Serve immediately.

SERVES 4
PREPARATION & COOKING TIME:
15 minutes + 20 minutes cooking
FREEZING: not recommended

ITALIAN STYLE BEANS ON TOASTED CIABATTA

A rather **gourmet version** of our traditional snack, beans on toast. None the less, the beans provide lots of soluble fibre with its cholesterol-lowering properties. Serve with a crisp green salad.

PER SERVING: 394 calories, 18 g fat

1 ciabatta loaf
2 tablespoons olive oil
130 g pack cubetti di pancetta
1 red onion, chopped finely
1 garlic clove, chopped finely
2 tablespoons tomato purée
400 g can of borlotti beans, rinsed and drained
400 g can of cannellini beans, rinsed and drained
2 large ripe tomatoes, de-seeded and chopped
2 tablespoons chopped fresh flat leaf parsley
freshly ground black pepper

1 Preheat the oven to Gas Mark 6/electric oven 200°C/fan oven 180°C.
2 Cut the ciabatta loaf in half lengthways, then cut each half into two equal pieces. Using 1 tablespoon of olive oil, brush the cut surfaces of the loaf. Place the four pieces of ciabatta on a baking sheet and bake in the oven for 5–10 minutes until lightly golden.
3 Heat the remaining tablespoon of oil in a large pan and cook the pancetta, red onion and garlic for 8–10 minutes until the onion is softened and the pancetta cooked. Stir in the tomato purée.
4 Add the beans and the chopped tomatoes. Simmer over a gentle heat for 5 minutes then stir in the chopped parsley and season well with freshly ground black pepper.
5 Arrange the slices of toasted ciabatta on warmed serving plates and spoon over the beans. Serve immediately.

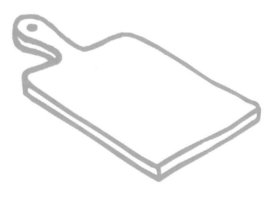

Fish really is good news for a healthy heart plan of eating! All fish can be eaten as frequently as you like, provided you do not deep fry it or smother it in rich, creamy sauces. As a minimum, we should have fish twice a week, with one of those helpings being an oily fish such as trout, salmon, tuna or mackerel for their heart-friendly omega-3 fatty acids.

FISH DISHES

The good thing is that we have an increasing choice of fish available to us as supermarkets now stock varieties such as swordfish, king-clip, mullet and monkfish as well as traditional favourites. An added bonus is that fish cooks quickly, so dinner can be on the table in no time at all after we come home from work.

SERVES 4
PREPARATION & COOKING TIME:
35 minutes
FREEZING: not recommended

PER SERVING: 412 calories, 30 g fat

The delicate shade of this sauce is perfect against the brighter colour of the pink salmon. However, its **rich nutritional value**, from the antioxidants and minerals in the watercress, is even more attractive. Also, using half fat crème fraîche in the sauce means that the fat content is kept as low as possible

SALMON WITH CRÈME FRAÎCHE & WATERCRESS SAUCE

4 x 150 g (5¹/₂ oz) pieces salmon fillet, skinned
I tablespoon vegetable oil plus extra for greasing
juice of ¹/₂ lemon

FOR THE SAUCE:
I tablespoon vegetable oil
3 shallots, chopped finely
I celery stick, trimmed and chopped finely
300 ml (¹/₂ pint) vegetable stock
75 g (2³/₄ oz) watercress, rough stalks removed
150 ml (¹/₄ pint) half fat crème fraîche
freshly ground black pepper

I Preheat the oven to Gas Mark 6/electric oven 200°C/fan oven 180°F.

2 To make the sauce, heat the oil in a pan and gently fry the shallots and celery for 4–5 minutes until softened. Pour in the stock, bring to the boil and bubble vigorously until the liquid is reduced by half.

3 Pour the mixture into a liquidiser and blend. Add the watercress and crème fraîche in stages, blending each time to create a smooth sauce. Return the sauce to the pan and reheat gently but do not allow to boil. Check the seasoning and add some freshly ground black pepper if required.

4 Place the salmon fillets on a lightly greased baking tray and brush with the vegetable oil. Sprinkle over the lemon juice. Bake in the oven for 10–15 minutes until the salmon is cooked. Serve immediately accompanied by the sauce.

SERVES 4
PREPARATION & COOKING TIME:
15 minutes + 30 minutes standing
+ 8 minutes cooking
FREEZING: not recommended

PER SERVING: 490 calories, 39 g fat

Swordfish, increasingly available although still fairly expensive, makes an excellent choice for a dinner party main course. It is **meaty and substantial** so can take quite robust flavourings. This warm dressing with olive oil, lemon juice and fresh herbs is an excellent accompaniment to the fish. Be careful not to overcook the steaks, they only need 3–4 minutes on each side. Serve with freshly boiled new potatoes and a green salad.

GRILLED SWORDFISH STEAKS WITH A WARM TOMATO & HERB DRESSING

4 swordfish steaks (about 175 g/ 6 oz each)
olive oil for brushing
freshly ground black pepper

FOR THE DRESSING:
2 large tomatoes, peeled, de-seeded and chopped
2 shallots, chopped finely
1 garlic clove, crushed
2 tablespoons chopped fresh chives
2 tablespoons chopped fresh flat leaf parsley
1 tablespoon roughly torn fresh basil
125 ml (4 fl oz) extra virgin olive oil
zest and juice of 1 lemon
freshly ground black pepper

1 Combine the tomatoes, shallots, garlic, herbs, olive oil and the lemon zest and juice in a bowl. Give a good grinding of black pepper, stir well and set aside for 30 minutes to allow the flavours to mingle.

2 Preheat the grill until hot. Place the swordfish steaks on a grill rack and brush each side with a little olive oil and season with freshly ground black pepper. Put under the heat and grill for 3–4 minutes each side. Do not allow to overcook and dry out.

3 While the fish is grilling, transfer the dressing to a small saucepan and warm through gently for 2–3 minutes.

4 Serve the swordfish steaks with the warmed dressing drizzled over each one.

SERVES 4–6
PREPARATION & COOKING TIME:
50 minutes + 1 hour chilling
FREEZING: not recommended

PER SERVING: 157 calories, 8 g fat

Savoury roulades are as good to enjoy as the sweet varieties and make an excellent main course **for a warm summer day**. Equally, an individual slice of roulade with a small salad garnish would make a very acceptable starter to a meal.

225 g (8 oz) broccoli florets
4 eggs, separated
a generous pinch of grated nutmeg
freshly ground black pepper

FOR THE FILLING:
200 g (7 oz) smoked salmon slices
200 g (7 oz) low fat cream cheese
2 tablespoons low fat plain yogurt
2 ripe tomatoes, peeled, de-seeded
and chopped finely
1 tablespoon snipped fresh chives

1 Preheat the oven to Gas Mark 7/electric oven 220°C/fan oven 200°C. Line a 33 × 23 cm (13 × 9 inch) Swiss roll tin with non-stick baking parchment.
2 Steam or gently simmer the broccoli florets until tender. Drain thoroughly, turn them on to a plate and chop finely. Place in a large mixing bowl with the egg yolks, the nutmeg and a grinding of black pepper. Mix well.
3 In a separate large bowl, whisk the egg whites until stiff but not dry. Stir 1 tablespoon of egg white into the broccoli mixture to loosen it slightly, then carefully fold in the remainder, taking care not to knock out any of the volume. Spread the broccoli mixture evenly into the prepared tin and bake in the oven for 10–12 minutes until firm and lightly golden.
4 Place a clean sheet of non-stick baking parchment on the work surface. Turn the roulade out on to the paper and leave to cool for 5 minutes. Peel off the lining paper and trim the edges of the roulade.
5 Carefully separate the slices of smoked salmon and lay them over the surface of the roulade. Mix together the cream cheese, yogurt, tomatoes and chives and spread in an even layer over the smoked salmon.
6 Using the sheet of baking parchment, roll up the roulade in the same way as a Swiss roll and, leaving it in the paper, chill in the fridge for about an hour to firm up. When ready to serve, remove the roulade from the paper and cut into thick slices.

BROCCOLI & SMOKED SALMON ROULADE

SERVES 4
PREPARATION & COOKING TIME:
20 minutes + 25 minutes cooking
FREEZING: not recommended

BAKED TROUT WITH LEMON & PARSLEY STUFFING

Trout, being an oily fish, should be one of those eaten at least once a week for its omega-3 fatty acids. This is a straightforward but **delicious way of cooking** the trout. It only needs a simple accompaniment of new potatoes and perhaps some lightly steamed mange tout.

PER SERVING: 530 calories, 33 g fat

2 tablespoons olive oil plus extra for greasing
4 medium trout, cleaned
freshly ground black pepper

FOR THE STUFFING:
125 g (4$^{1}/_{2}$ oz) fresh white breadcrumbs
2 tablespoons chopped fresh parsley
2 garlic cloves, chopped finely
grated zest and juice of 2 lemons
4 tablespoons olive oil

1   Preheat the oven to Gas Mark 5/electric oven 190°C/fan oven 170°C.
2   Lightly grease a roasting tin large enough to hold the four trout.
3   To prepare the stuffing, place the breadcrumbs, parsley, garlic and grated lemon zest in a bowl. Stir in the olive oil and 1 tablespoon of lemon juice. Season with black pepper and mix well to combine the ingredients.
4   Divide the stuffing evenly between the cavities of the four trout. Place the trout side by side in the roasting tin.
5   In a small bowl, whisk together 2 tablespoons of olive oil and a further tablespoon of lemon juice. Season lightly with black pepper and drizzle the dressing over the trout.
6   Bake in the oven for 20–25 minutes or until the fish is cooked. Serve immediately, spooning any pan juices over the trout.

SERVES 4
PREPARATION & COOKING TIME: 30 minutes
FREEZING: not recommended

CHARGRILLED TUNA WITH MEXICAN STYLE SALSA

Tuna is a firm, substantial fish and the flavour of cooked, fresh tuna is **far superior to the tinned variety.** Just be careful not to overcook it otherwise it becomes rather dry.

PER SERVING: 305 calories, 14 g fat

4 fresh tuna steaks
1 tablespoon olive oil

FOR THE SALSA:
1 ripe avocado, stoned, peeled and diced
1 garlic clove, chopped finely
2 tomatoes, peeled, de-seeded and diced
198 g can of sweetcorn, drained
1 fresh green chilli, de-seeded and diced finely
grated zest and juice of 2 limes
1 tablespoon chopped fresh parsley

1   To make the salsa, combine all the salsa ingredients in a small bowl and stir well to coat with the lime juice. Set aside to allow the flavours to develop.
2   Brush the tuna steaks on each side with the olive oil. Heat a ridged griddle pan or frying pan until very hot and cook the tuna steaks for about 5 minutes on each side, depending on their thickness.
3   Serve the tuna immediately accompanied by the salsa.

SERVES 4
PREPARATION & COOKING TIME: 25 minutes
FREEZING: not recommended

SMOKED MACKEREL & PASTA SALAD

A **colourful, crunchy salad** and an interesting way to use smoked mackerel. Do remember that smoked fish have a higher salt content and so it is unlikely that you will need to add salt to the salad dressing – a good grinding of black pepper will be sufficient. Serve with some warmed crusty bread.

PER SERVING: 772 calories, 57 g fat

150 g (5¹/₂ oz) dried fusilli pasta
4 smoked mackerel fillets, skinned and flaked
1 bunch of spring onions, trimmed and sliced
1 pink grapefruit, peeled and segmented
1 red apple, cored and chopped
2 celery sticks, trimmed and sliced
1 small bag of mixed salad leaves

FOR THE DRESSING:
125 ml (4 fl oz) extra virgin olive oil
4 tablespoons white wine vinegar
1 dessertspoon clear honey
1 tablespoon coarse-grain mustard
freshly ground black pepper

1   Cook the pasta in a large pan of boiling water for 10 minutes, or according to the packet instructions, until 'al dente'. Drain and rinse thoroughly with cold water to cool the pasta quickly.
2   Put the pasta, mackerel, spring onions, grapefruit, apple and celery in a large mixing bowl and stir gently to combine.
3   Make the dressing by putting all the ingredients into a screw top jar and shaking vigorously, or place in a small bowl and whisk well. Pour the dressing over the salad ingredients and mix well.
4   Spread the salad leaves on a large serving plate and pile the salad mixture on top. Serve immediately.

SERVES 4
PREPARATION & COOKING TIME:
25 minutes + 20 minutes cooking
FREEZING: not recommended

ORIENTAL COD PARCELS

Individual foil parcels means that the cod stays wonderfully moist, almost steaming in the flavoursome dressing. Remember that white fish, provided it is not cooked with a lot of fat, is a good low calorie source of protein, vitamins and minerals. Serve the baked cod portions on a bed of mixed long grain and wild rice.

PER SERVING: 235 calories, 5 g fat

4 x 150–175 g (4¹/₂–5¹/₂ oz) boneless, skinless cod fillets
1 carrot, cut into matchsticks
1 courgette, trimmed and cut into matchsticks
1 yellow pepper, de-seeded and sliced thinly
4 spring onions, trimmed and shredded
2.5 cm (1 inch) piece of fresh root ginger, peeled and sliced thinly

FOR THE DRESSING:
3 tablespoons reduced salt soy sauce
4 tablespoons dry sherry
1 tablespoon sesame oil
1 tablespoon clear honey

1   Preheat the oven to Gas Mark 6/electric oven 200°C/fan oven 180°C and cut four large squares of foil.
2   Place one cod fillet in the centre of each foil square and scatter the prepared vegetables and ginger evenly over the top of the fish portions. Ease up the edges of the foil to create a container.
3   In a small bowl or measuring jug, mix together the ingredients for the dressing with 2 tablespoons of cold water. Pour the dressing over each portion of cod and vegetables. Scrunch together the top edges of the foil to form parcels and place the parcels on two baking sheets.
4   Bake in the oven for 15–20 minutes until the fish is cooked and flakes easily and the vegetables are just tender. Remove the fish and vegetables from the parcels and serve.

SERVES 4
PREPARATION & COOKING TIME:
20 minutes + 20 minutes cooking
FREEZING: not recommended

PER SERVING: 463 calories, 31 g fat

4 x 150–175 g (5½–6 oz) boneless, skinless
salmon fillets

FOR THE CRUST:
75 g (2¾ oz) fresh white breadcrumbs
finely grated zest of ½ lemon
25 g (1 oz) stoned black olives,
chopped finely
25 g (1 oz) sunblush tomatoes,
chopped finely
1 tablespoon finely chopped
fresh flat leaf parsley
2 tablespoons olive oil

FOR THE ROASTED TOMATOES:
1 pack of small tomatoes on the vine
1 tablespoon olive oil
freshly ground black pepper

The crispness of the topping contrasts well with the softer texture of the fish, and the roasted tomatoes prevent the dish from being dry. Use **sunblush or semi-cuit tomatoes** for this recipe in preference to sun-dried tomatoes, because they are brighter in colour and also more moist.

1   Preheat the oven to Gas Mark 6/electric oven 200°C/fan oven 180°C. Line a baking sheet with non-stick baking parchment and place the salmon fillets on it.
2   In a small bowl, mix together the breadcrumbs, lemon zest, olives, sunblush tomatoes and parsley. Add the olive oil and stir well to moisten the breadcrumbs and combine the ingredients.
3   Spoon the breadcrumb mixture evenly over the salmon pieces and press it down lightly to form a crust. Bake in the oven for 15–20 minutes until the salmon is cooked and the breadcrumbs lightly golden and crusty.
4   Meanwhile, place the vine tomatoes, still on the stalk, in a small roasting tin. Drizzle over the olive oil and give them a grinding of black pepper. Bake in the oven for 10–15 minutes along with the fish until just tender and softened.
5   To serve, place a salmon portion on a warmed plate and top each one with a few of the tomatoes still on their vine.

OLIVE & SUNBLUSH TOMATO CRUSTED SALMON WITH ROASTED VINE TOMATOES

Eating for a healthy heart doesn't mean avoiding red meat – indeed, it is a valuable source of protein and iron. However, it does mean, perhaps, being slightly wise and choosing leaner cuts, removing all the visible fat when preparing it for cooking, and switching to cooking methods such as stir frying or grilling which use the minimum of fat. With a non-stick pan you can use the smallest amount of oil when sealing meat for a casserole or even cook the meat in its own fat then add the sauce ingredients for flavour and moisture.

Poultry, on the other hand, is an obvious choice for low fat eating, with much

MEAT & POULTRY

of the fat it does contain being low in saturates. Again, it is a matter of choosing wise cooking methods and removing the skin before eating or, preferably, before cooking.

The recipes in this chapter make good family eating, with none of them too complicated to prepare. Where possible, I have added lots of veggies and pulses into the cooking, but using canned varieties of beans and lentils so that you don't have to think about soaking and long cooking times. Trying the wonderful flavours of the Sausage Casserole with Red Wine & Puy Lentils may make you reconsider the role of the humble lentil!

SERVES 4
PREPARATION & COOKING TIME:
15 minutes + 2 hours marinating + 35 minutes cooking
FREEZING: not recommended

SPICY CHICKEN ON A BED OF COUSCOUS

This dish is based on the wonderfully warming North African **harissa paste**. If you have never used it before, the quantity in this recipe will give a medium spiciness. Once you have gauged its strength you can adjust to suit your own preference. Jars of harissa paste are found in most of the large supermarkets.

PER SERVING: 396 calories, 8 g fat

4 skinless, boneless chicken breasts
150 ml ('/4 pint) low fat plain yogurt
juice of 1 lemon
2 teaspoons harissa paste
'/2 teaspoon ground cumin
'/2 teaspoon ground coriander
fresh coriander leaves, to garnish (optional)

FOR THE COUSCOUS:
300 g (10'/2 oz) couscous
500ml (18 fl oz) hot chicken stock
1 tablespoon olive oil
1 red onion, chopped
1 fresh red chilli, de-seeded and chopped finely
1 garlic clove, crushed
1 red pepper, de-seeded and diced
3 tablespoons finely chopped fresh coriander
freshly ground black pepper

1   Make three slashes in the top surface of each chicken breast and place them in a shallow dish.
2   Mix together the yogurt, 1 tablespoon of lemon juice, the harissa paste, cumin and coriander and pour over the chicken pieces, coating them completely. Cover and place in the fridge to marinate for 2 hours, turning them once.
3   Preheat the oven to Gas Mark 6/electric oven 200°C/fan oven 180°C.
4   Lift the chicken pieces out of the marinade and place them in a small roasting tin. Bake in the oven for 30–35 minutes until the chicken is thoroughly cooked and lightly browned on top.
5   Meanwhile, place the couscous in a large bowl and pour over the hot stock, stirring once or twice to prevent any dry pockets of grains. Leave aside for 10 minutes to allow the couscous to swell and absorb the stock.
6   Heat the olive oil in a frying pan and gently fry the onion for 5–6 minutes until softened. Stir in the chilli, garlic and red pepper and continue to cook for a further 5 minutes. Stir this into the hot couscous along with the chopped fresh coriander and a grinding of black pepper.
7   Divide the couscous mixture equally between four serving plates. Remove the chicken from the oven and place each portion on a bed of couscous. Garnish with some whole coriander leaves if desired and serve immediately.

SERVES 6
PREPARATION & COOKING TIME:
40 minutes + 20 minutes cooking
FREEZING: not recommended

TURKEY & LEEK FILO TOPPED PIE

Following a healthy eating pattern means avoiding traditional pastry dishes, which are usually very high in fat. However, it's hard to do without completely and this is where **filo pastry** comes into its own. Instead of brushing it with melted butter, as many recipes instruct, use a small amount of vegetable or olive oil – or even no oil at all, since the pastry still bakes to an attractive golden colour.

PER SERVING: 422 calories, 9 g fat

2 tablespoons vegetable oil
750 g (1 lb 10oz) turkey breast pieces, cubed
2 leeks, trimmed and sliced into rings
2 celery sticks, sliced
1 onion, sliced
2 small carrots, sliced
2 tablespoons plain flour
150 ml ($^1/_4$ pint) dry cider
300 ml ($^1/_2$ pint) chicken stock
1 tablespoon Dijon mustard
2 tablespoons half fat crème fraîche
freshly ground black pepper
6 sheets filo pastry
1 teaspoon sesame seeds

1 Preheat the oven to Gas Mark 6/electric oven 200°C/fan oven 180°C.
2 Heat 1 tablespoon of the oil in a large pan and fry the turkey cubes in batches until golden brown. Set aside. Add the vegetables to the pan and gently sauté for 4–5 minutes. Sprinkle over the flour and cook for 1 minute.
3 Gradually stir in the cider and stock, followed by the mustard and bring up to the boil, stirring to allow the sauce to thicken. Return the turkey to the pan. Reduce the heat, cover the pan and simmer gently for 15–20 minutes until the vegetables are tender. Stir in the crème fraîche and season with black pepper. Transfer the mixture to a shallow ovenproof dish.
4 Take one sheet of filo pastry at a time, spread it out on a clean work surface and lightly brush with the remaining oil. Crumple each sheet slightly and arrange on top of the turkey mixture to cover it completely. Sprinkle over the sesame seeds.
5 Place the pie in the oven and bake for 15–20 minutes until the pastry is golden brown and crisp. Serve immediately.

SERVES 4
PREPARATION & COOKING TIME:
45 minutes
FREEZING: not recommended

PER SERVING: 493 calories, 11 g fat

Traditional Mexican fajitas are very tasty but, with the guacamole, soured cream and grated cheese, can also be very high in fat. I have developed this **healthier version** of fajitas which is brilliant served with a crisp green salad and some low fat home made potato wedges.

TURKEY & SWEET PEPPER WRAPS WITH POTATO WEDGES

FOR THE POTATO WEDGES:
3 medium to large baking potatoes
1 teaspoon paprika
$^1/_2$ tablespoon olive oil
freshly ground black pepper

FOR THE WRAPS:
1 tablespoon olive oil
500 g (1 lb 2 oz) thinly sliced turkey breast, cut into strips
1 red onion, sliced
2 garlic cloves, crushed
1 red pepper, de-seeded and sliced
1 green pepper, de-seeded and sliced
1 teaspoon paprika
$^1/_4$ teaspoon chilli powder
200 g can of chopped tomatoes
4 flour tortilla wraps
150 g pot of no fat Greek yogurt
$1^1/_2$ tablespoons reduced fat green pesto sauce

1　To make the wedges, preheat the oven to Gas Mark 5/electric oven 190°C/fan oven 170°C.

2　Wash and dry the potatoes but do not peel them. Cut each one in half lengthways, then cut each half into four wedges. Place in a large mixing bowl and sprinkle over the paprika, olive oil and black pepper. Stir well to coat the wedges evenly. Tip them on to a baking sheet, spread out and then bake for about 35 minutes until golden and tender.

3　To make the wraps, heat the oil in a large frying pan and cook the strips of turkey breast over a moderate heat until browned and cooked through. Transfer to a plate and set aside.

4　Add the onion, garlic and peppers to the pan and cook for 5–6 minutes until just tender. Stir in the paprika, chilli powder and chopped tomatoes. Mix well and bring up to simmering point. Return the turkey to the pan and simmer for about 10 minutes, stirring occasionally.

5　Meanwhile, wrap the tortillas in foil and place in the oven to warm through for 8–10 minutes.

6　Mix together the Greek yogurt and the pesto. Divide the mixture evenly between the warmed tortillas and spread almost to the edge. Place equal quantities of the turkey and pepper mixture down the centre of each tortilla. Roll up and serve immediately, accompanied by the potato wedges.

SERVES 4
PREPARATION & COOKING TIME:
20 minutes + 30 minutes cooking
FREEZING: not recommended

PER SERVING: 391 calories, 13 g fat

This recipe allows a small amount of cooked ham to serve four people with a generous helping and is **ideal for using up any ham** left over at Christmas time. Although half fat cheeses were rather rubbery and tasteless when they first appeared, they have now improved greatly in flavour and cooking qualities. Serve with a selection of lightly cooked green vegetables or a crisp green salad.

BACON & TOMATO PASTA BAKE

175 g (6 oz) dried fusilli pasta
1 tablespoon vegetable oil
1 onion, chopped
2 garlic cloves, chopped
200 g (7 oz) cooked ham, cubed
400 g can of chopped tomatoes
1 teaspoon dried basil
300 ml (¹/₂ pint) semi skimmed milk
2 eggs
1 tablespoon tomato purée
freshly ground black pepper
75 g (2³/₄ oz) half fat mature
Cheddar cheese, grated

1 Preheat the oven to Gas Mark 4/electric oven 180°C/fan oven 160°C.

2 Cook the pasta in boiling water for about 10 minutes, or according to the packet instructions, until 'al dente'. Drain thoroughly.

3 Meanwhile, heat the vegetable oil in a large frying pan and fry the onion and garlic for 5 minutes to soften. Add the cubed ham, tomatoes and dried basil. Simmer for 8–10 minutes.

4 Stir the cooked pasta gently into the bacon and tomato mixture and stir gently to combine. Turn the mixture into a shallow ovenproof dish.

5 Whisk together the milk, eggs and tomato purée. Season with freshly ground black pepper. Pour the egg mixture over the pasta and sprinkle the grated Cheddar over the top.

6 Place in the oven and bake for 25–30 minutes until the mixture is set and the top is golden brown. Serve immediately.

SERVES 4
PREPARATION & COOKING TIME:
15 minutes + 1 hour cooking
FREEZING: recommended

PER SERVING: 412 calories, 18 g fat

A superior sausage casserole which is flavoursome enough to serve at an informal dinner party. Using a good quality low fat sausage and the soluble fibre from the lentils makes this a much healthier option to the traditional sausage casserole. Serve with mashed potatoes and lightly steamed Savoy cabbage.

1 tablespoon olive oil
454 g pack of good quality reduced fat sausages
1 onion, sliced
2 garlic cloves, crushed
1 teaspoon ground allspice
1/2 teaspoon ground nutmeg
2 x 400 g cans of chopped tomatoes
2 sprigs of rosemary
2 bay leaves
200 ml (7 fl oz) red wine
100 g (3 1/2 oz) Puy lentils

1 Heat the oil in a large sauté pan or flameproof casserole and cook the sausages for 5–8 minutes until nicely browned all over. Remove from the pan and set aside.
2 Add the onion and garlic to the pan and cook gently until the onion is softened. Stir in the allspice and the nutmeg and mix well.
3 Pour in the tomatoes and bring to the boil. Simmer for 4–5 minutes to thicken slightly then add the rosemary, bay leaves, red wine and Puy lentils. Stir in 200 ml (7 fl oz) cold water. Return the sausages to the pan and bring back up to the boil.
4 Cover the pan and reduce the heat. Simmer for 35–40 minutes until the lentils are tender. Stir several times during the cooking to prevent the lentils sticking to the base of the pan, and add a little more water if the sauce is becoming too thick. Remove the rosemary sprigs and the bay leaves before serving.

SAUSAGE CASSEROLE WITH RED WINE & PUY LENTILS

SERVES 4
PREPARATION & COOKING TIME:
10 minutes + 40 minutes cooking
FREEZING: recommended

SERVES 4
PREPARATION & COOKING TIME:
15 minutes + 1 hour marinating + 30 minutes cooking
FREEZING: recommended

CHICKEN WITH SMOKY BACON & CANNELLINI BEANS

STICKY GLAZED DRUMSTICKS

A quick to prepare recipe suitable for **a midweek evening meal** – it only needs to be accompanied by boiled new potatoes and some lightly steamed broccoli. Although the excess fat should be removed from the bacon, there should still be sufficient rendered out in the heat of the pan to cook off the onion and garlic – so don't be tempted to add any oil.

PER SERVING: 265 calories, 6 g fat

1 onion, chopped
4 rashers smoked, reduced salt back bacon, chopped
1 garlic clove, chopped
4 boneless, skinless chicken breasts, cubed
400 g can of chopped tomatoes
1 teaspoon dried thyme
1 teaspoon paprika
410 g can of cannellini beans, rinsed and drained
freshly ground black pepper
chopped fresh parsley, to garnish

1 Gently fry the chopped onion, bacon and garlic in a large pan for 5–6 minutes to soften the onion and cook the bacon. Add the cubed chicken to the pan and continue to cook until the chicken is sealed and lightly golden.
2 Stir in the chopped tomatoes along with the thyme and paprika. Bring up to the boil, then cover and reduce the heat. Simmer for 20–25 minutes, stirring occasionally.
3 Add the cannellini beans to the pan and stir into the mixture. Cook for a further 10 minutes until the beans are heated through and the chicken cooked. Season to taste with freshly ground black pepper. Serve immediately, sprinkled with some chopped parsley as a garnish.

A supremely simple, but tasty way to liven up chicken drumsticks or thighs – but be sure to remove the fatty skin before marinating. Equally **delicious served hot or cold**.

PER SERVING: 425 calories, 21 g fat

8 chicken drumsticks or thighs or a mixture of each, skin removed

FOR THE MARINADE:
zest and juice of 1 orange
2 tablespoons clear honey
2 tablespoons olive oil
$1/2$ teaspoon ground ginger
$1/2$ teaspoon ground cumin
1 tablespoon orange marmalade
freshly ground black pepper

1 Place the chicken pieces in a shallow dish. Whisk together all the ingredients for the marinade, ensuring that the marmalade is well broken up.
2 Pour the marinade over the chicken pieces and turn them to coat well. Place in the fridge and leave for at least an hour to allow the flavours to develop.
3 Preheat the oven to Gas Mark 4/electric oven 180°C/fan oven 160°C.
4 Remove the chicken pieces from the marinade and place in a shallow roasting tin. Drizzle over a little of the marinade and then discard the rest.
5 Roast the chicken pieces for 25–30 minutes until thoroughly cooked. When the chicken is pierced, any juices should be completely clear and not tinged with pink. Serve hot or cold.

SERVES 4
PREPARATION & COOKING TIME:
25 minutes + 1½ hours cooking
FREEZING: recommended

BEEF IN RED WINE

This **elegant casserole** could be used for a dinner party, and if prepared the day beforehand then kept in the fridge the flavour will develop and enrich. Remember to use as lean a braising steak as possible and cut off any excess visible fat.

PER SERVING: 321 calories, 12 g fat

500 g (1 lb 2 oz) lean braising steak, cubed
25 g (1 oz) seasoned flour
1 tablespoon vegetable oil
1 large onion, sliced
2 garlic cloves, crushed
2 carrots, sliced
2 celery sticks, trimmed and sliced
300 ml (½ pint) beef stock
300 ml (½ pint) red wine
1 teaspoon dried thyme
2 bay leaves
2 tablespoons tomato purée
225 g (8 oz) closed cup mushrooms, quartered
freshly ground black pepper

1 Preheat the oven to Gas Mark 3/electric oven 170°C/fan oven 150°C.
2 Toss the cubed beef in the seasoned flour to coat lightly. Heat the oil in a frying pan and fry off batches of the beef to brown and seal. Using a slotted spoon, transfer the beef to a casserole dish.
3 Add the onion, garlic, carrots and celery to the pan and cook gently for 5–6 minutes until softened. Pour in the beef stock and red wine and add the thyme, bay leaves and tomato purée. Stir to disperse the tomato purée and bring the mixture up to the boil.
4 Pour the liquid into the casserole dish and mix well with the beef. Cover the casserole and cook in the oven for 1¼ hours. Stir the mushrooms into the casserole and return to the oven for a further 15 minutes or until the beef is very tender. Check the seasoning and serve immediately.

SERVES 4
PREPARATION & COOKING TIME:
35 minutes
FREEZING: not recommended

PER SERVING: 208 calories, 8 g fat

350 g (12 oz) lean rump steak, sliced finely
1¹/₂ teaspoons Chinese five spice powder
2 teaspoons cornflour
1 tablespoon vegetable oil
1 onion, sliced
1 garlic clove, chopped finely
1 fresh red chilli, de-seeded
and chopped finely
4 cm (1¹/₂ inch) piece of fresh root ginger,
peeled and chopped finely
1 red pepper, de-seeded and sliced
1 green pepper, de-seeded and sliced
125 g (4¹/₂ oz) baby sweetcorn,
sliced on the diagonal
150 ml (¹/₄ pint) beef stock
3 tablespoons oyster sauce
3 spring onions, sliced finely
freshly ground black pepper

Stir frying is an excellent cooking method for retaining the maximum amount of nutrients in the food. Although cooked at high temperatures, the whole process takes no more than a few minutes so vegetables stay crunchy and valuable vitamins and minerals are not lost. Always prepare the ingredients before starting to cook to ensure that cooking flows as rapidly as possible. Serve with cooked noodles or rice.

1   Toss the sliced rump steak with the five spice powder and cornflour to coat the meat. Set aside.
2   Heat the oil in a wok or large frying pan and stir fry the onion slices for 2 minutes. Add the garlic, chilli and root ginger and fry for a further minute. Finally, add the sliced peppers and baby sweetcorn and stir fry until the vegetables are just tender – no more than 3–4 minutes. Transfer the vegetables to a plate and keep warm.
3   Add the sliced beef to the wok and stir fry to brown the beef completely. Pour in the stock and the oyster sauce and cook for about 2 minutes until the stock thickens slightly. Season with freshly ground black pepper.
4   Return the vegetables to the wok and stir fry for a further 2 minutes until everything is heated through. Take care not to overcook. Serve the stir fry immediately, sprinkled with the sliced spring onions.

SPICY BEEF STIR FRY

SERVES 4
PREPARATION & COOKING TIME:
40 minutes + 15 minutes cooking
FREEZING: not recommended

PER SERVING: 270 calories, 15 g fat

This recipe was developed by my daughter Kathryn for her GCSE Food Technology brief, when she had to create a healthy main course which would appeal to teenagers. It has become a **family favourite** ever since. Grilling the lamb burgers removes a lot of the fat from the meat although, if you prefer an even healthier option, the recipe is equally successful using turkey mince for the burgers. The burgers are delicious served with the salsa on a bed of warm flavoured couscous and accompanied by some mixed salad leaves.

MILDLY SPICED LAMB BURGERS WITH MANGO SALSA

FOR THE BURGERS:
450 g (1 lb) minced lamb
zest and juice of 1 lime
1 tablespoon chopped fresh coriander leaves
$^1/_2$ teaspoon ground cumin
$^1/_2$ teaspoon ground allspice
1 small onion, chopped very finely
freshly ground black pepper

FOR THE SALSA:
1 large ripe mango, peeled and diced
100 g (3$^1/_2$ oz) cherry tomatoes, quartered
$^1/_2$ small red onion, finely chopped
zest and juice of 1 lime
2 tablespoons chopped fresh coriander leaves
1 cm ($^1/_2$ inch) piece of fresh root ginger, peeled and grated
freshly ground black pepper

1 Put all the ingredients for the burgers into a large bowl and mix together until well combined. Divide into four, and shape each into a burger about 2.5 cm (1 inch) thick. Put the burgers on a plate, cover with clingfilm and chill for 30 minutes.

2 Meanwhile, carefully stir together the ingredients for the salsa then set aside to allow the flavours to develop.

3 Preheat the grill until hot. Place the burgers on the rack of the grill pan and grill for about 12–15 minutes, turning occasionally, until the burgers are thoroughly cooked through, with no hint of pink in the centre. Serve immediately, accompanied by the salsa.

SERVES 4
PREPARATION & COOKING TIME:
35 minutes
FREEZING: not recommended

PER SERVING: 665 calories, 33 g fat

This is based on a wonderful **French recipe** which normally uses lashings of butter and cream. This much healthier version tastes equally delicious but contains about half the fat. Don't be tempted to use English mustard instead of the Dijon, because it is far too fiery and would completely spoil the sauce. However, a good quality dry cider could be used instead of the white wine, to give the recipe a hint of flavours from Normandy. Serve the chops accompanied by some boiled new potatoes and a selection of lightly steamed vegetables.

PORK CHOPS WITH A CREAMY DIJONNAISE SAUCE

1 tablespoon sunflower oil
4 large pork loin chops,
all visible fat removed
freshly ground black pepper
100 ml (3½ fl oz) dry white wine
1 teaspoon dried thyme
150 ml (¼ pint) half fat crème fraîche
1 teaspoon tomato purée
1 tablespoon Dijon mustard
1 tomato, peeled, de-seeded and diced
1 tablespoon chopped fresh parsley

1 Heat the oil in a large frying pan. Season the pork chops with freshly ground black pepper and add to the pan. Seal quickly on both sides then reduce the heat. Cook the chops for a further 3 minutes each side then remove from the pan to a plate. Pour off all the excess fat and wipe out the pan with kitchen towel.

2 Return the pan to the heat and pour in the wine and thyme. Bubble vigorously for 2–3 minutes until the wine is reduced to about one third of its original volume. Stir in the crème fraîche and tomato purée then return the pork chops to the pan. Cook the chops for 5–6 minutes over a medium heat until tender, being careful not to overcook.

3 Stir in the Dijon mustard, diced tomato and chopped parsley. Continue to cook for a further 2–3 minutes until heated through. Serve the chops immediately, with the sauce.

Vegetables play an important role in any healthy eating plan, and we are very lucky to have such a huge variety of fresh vegetables available to us these days. There are wonderfully shaped and coloured squashes, such as the butternut, for roasting or adding to casseroles, and exotic oriental mushrooms, full of heart-healthy vitamins and minerals – for speedy main course cooking nothing could beat the Oriental Braised Mushrooms. There is almost no limit to just how tasty and satisfying meat-free main courses can be.

VEGETARIAN

Apart from being packed with essential nutrients and fibre, veggies mix well with grains such as rice and couscous, are delicious with pasta and, when used with filo pastry in the Carrot, Cashew & Chestnut Pie or the Mediterranean Roasted Vegetable Strudel recipes, make excellent low fat pastry options.

It's a good thing to have a meat-free day every now and again, and with the choice from these recipes you won't be stuck for an idea.

SERVES 4
PREPARATION & COOKING TIME:
45 minutes
FREEZING: not recommended

PER SERVING: 465 calories, 7 g fat

Risottos make very simple yet elegant meals and are not as difficult to cook successfully as many believe. A basic risotto is a wonderful vehicle for all sorts of additions, and here I have used a **mixture of fresh summer vegetables** to help ensure a good supply of vitamins and antioxidants. Accompany with a crisp salad, if desired.

1 tablespoon olive oil
1 onion, chopped
2 garlic cloves, chopped
100 g (3½ oz) asparagus tips
1 courgette, sliced
350 g (12 oz) risotto rice
300 ml (½ pint) dry white wine
1 litre (1¾ pints) hot vegetable stock
125 g (4½ oz) shelled broad beans, defrosted if using frozen
2 ripe tomatoes, de-seeded and chopped
2 tablespoons chopped fresh parsley
1 tablespoon roughly torn fresh basil
25 g (1 oz) Parmesan cheese, freshly grated
freshly ground black pepper

1 Heat the oil in a large frying pan and gently cook the onion and garlic for 3–4 minutes until softened but not coloured. Transfer to a plate using a slotted spoon. Add the asparagus tips and courgette slices to the pan and cook for 3–4 minutes. Remove to the plate and keep warm.

2 Add the risotto rice and cook for about 1 minute, stirring, to allow the grains to become coated with the oil. Pour in the wine, bring up to the boil, then reduce the heat and simmer gently, stirring until the wine has been absorbed.

3 Add half the hot vegetable stock and bring to the boil. Again, reduce the heat and simmer gently, stirring until the stock is absorbed. Add half of the remaining stock along with the broad beans. Bring to the boil and then allow to simmer gently until the liquid is absorbed.

4 Add the last of the stock and bring to the boil, Simmer gently until the stock is absorbed and the rice is tender. As a guide, the whole process of adding stock and simmering to cook the rice should take no more than about 25 minutes. If it has taken less time then the rice may not be thoroughly cooked but if it takes longer, then the rice is being overcooked. The consistency of the risotto should be thick and creamy with the grains of rice soft but still retaining a little bite.

5 Stir in the tomatoes, herbs and the reserved vegetables along with the Parmesan and some freshly ground black pepper. Mix gently. Remove from the heat, cover the pan and leave to stand for 4–5 minutes to allow the flavours to mix. Serve on warmed plates.

SUMMER VEGETABLE RISOTTO

SERVES 4
PREPARATION & COOKING TIME:
20 minutes + 25 minutes cooking
FREEZING: not recommended

PER SERVING: 156 calories, 8 g fat

This pasta sauce is based on a **Neapolitan style of ratatouille**. It has lovely robust flavours and a richness from the red wine. When preparing the vegetables, chop them into chunky pieces. I think it serves well with tagliatelle, as the vegetable pieces nestle in attractively amongst the strands of pasta.

2 tablespoons olive oil
I onion, sliced
2 garlic cloves, chopped finely
I aubergine, cut into bite size pieces
I red or yellow pepper, de-seeded and cut into cubes
2 courgettes, cut into chunky rounds
I bulb of fennel, root and fronds removed, and cut into 6 wedges
400 g can of chopped tomatoes
150 ml ('/4 pint) red wine
I teaspoon fennel seeds, lightly crushed
I teaspoon dried oregano
I tablespoon tomato purée
125 g (4'/2 oz) closed cap mushrooms, quartered
freshly ground black pepper

1   Heat the olive oil in a large saucepan and gently fry the onion for about 5 minutes to soften. Add the chopped garlic and cook for a further minute.
2   Add the prepared vegetables (apart from the mushrooms), the chopped tomatoes, red wine, fennel seeds and oregano. Stir to mix well, bring up to the boil and then reduce the heat, cover and simmer gently for 15–20 minutes.
3   Stir in the mushrooms and continue to cook for a further 5–8 minutes or until the vegetables are just tender. Season to taste with black pepper and serve immediately with freshly cooked pasta.

CHUNKY VEGETABLE & TOMATO PASTA SAUCE

SERVES 4
PREPARATION & COOKING TIME:
1 hour
FREEZING: not recommended

PER SERVING: 408 calories, 21 g fat

This strudel is bursting with **Mediterranean flavours**, and using filo pastry keeps the fat content low. Serve in thick slices with new potatoes and a crisp green salad.

1 red pepper, de-seeded and diced
1 orange pepper, de-seeded and diced
1 aubergine, cubed
2 small red onions, quartered
2 courgettes, trimmed and thickly sliced
4 garlic cloves
3 tablespoons olive oil
1 teaspoon dried thyme
freshly ground black pepper
100 g (3$^1/_2$ oz) Feta cheese, cubed
1 tablespoon balsamic vinegar

FOR THE PASTRY:
5 large sheets of filo pastry
1 tablespoon olive oil

3 sprigs of fresh thyme to garnish

1 Preheat the oven to Gas Mark 7/electric oven 220°C/fan oven 200°C.
2 Place the prepared peppers, aubergine, onions, courgettes and garlic cloves in a large roasting tin. Drizzle over the olive oil and stir well to ensure the vegetables are thoroughly coated. Sprinkle over the thyme and season with black pepper.
3 Roast in the oven for 20–25 minutes until the vegetables are tender and the edges just beginning to char. Remove from the oven and leave aside to cool for about 10 minutes. When cool, carefully stir in the Feta cheese and balsamic vinegar.
4 Reduce the oven temperature to Gas Mark 5/electric oven 190°C/fan oven 170°C. Place a sheet of non-stick baking parchment on a baking sheet measuring 33 x 23 cm (13 x 9 inches).
5 Lay one sheet of filo pastry on a clean work surface and lightly brush with a little of the olive oil. Lay the second sheet on top of the first and lightly brush with oil. Repeat the process with the remaining sheets.
6 Carefully spread the roasted vegetable mixture over the pastry, leaving a border of 2.5 cm (1 inch) around the edges. Fold over each short end and then roll up the pastry lengthways like a Swiss roll. Ensure the short ends remain tucked in. Transfer carefully to the baking sheet, making sure that the seam is underneath. Lightly brush the top surface of the pastry with any remaining oil. Using a sharp knife make light diagonal slashes across the top of the pastry.
7 Place in the oven and bake for 20–25 minutes until the pastry is crisp and golden. Remove from the oven and cut into thick slices to serve.

MEDITERRANEAN ROASTED VEGETABLE STRUDEL

SERVES 4
PREPARATION TIME: 25 minutes
FREEZING: not recommended

COUSCOUS SALAD WITH MIXED BEANS, FETA CHEESE & OLIVES

This recipe, with the Feta cheese and black olives, is **inspired by Greek flavours**. While it does include cheese, Feta is not one of the highest in fat content and has a fresh crumbly texture. However, it can be fairly salty, as are the olives from soaking in brine, but just make sure you rinse the olives well and don't add any additional salt to the recipe.

PER SERVING: 540 calories, 27 g fat

250 g (9 oz) couscous
350 ml (12 fl oz) boiling water
400 g can of chick peas, rinsed and drained
400 g can of borlotti beans, rinsed and drained
200 g (7 oz) cherry tomatoes, halved
100 g (3¹/₂ oz) stoned black olives, rinsed and drained
200 g (7 oz) Feta cheese, cubed
2 tablespoons chopped fresh mint
2 tablespoons chopped fresh flat leaf parsley
3 tablespoons extra virgin olive oil
3 tablespoons freshly squeezed lemon juice
freshly ground black pepper

1   Place the couscous in a large bowl and pour over the boiling water. Stir, then leave to stand for 10 minutes to allow the grains to swell and absorb the water. Finally, fork through to loosen up the couscous.
2   Gently stir in all the other ingredients and mix well to combine. Season to taste with black pepper and transfer to a large serving dish. It can be lightly chilled before serving and will keep for 2 days in the fridge in an airtight container.

SERVES 4
PREPARATION & COOKING TIME: 30 minutes
FREEZING: not recommended

ORIENTAL BRAISED MUSHROOMS

Mushrooms are a **good source of protein** and are extremely low in calories as long as they are not cooked in rich, creamy sauces. Oriental mushrooms, especially the shiitake, contain elements that are thought to help in lowering blood pressure and blood cholesterol levels and so are useful in maintaining a healthy cardiovascular system.

PER SERVING: 218 calories, 6 g fat

1 tablespoon vegetable oil
2 garlic cloves, chopped
125 g (4¹/₂ oz) shiitake mushrooms, thickly sliced
125 g (4¹/₂ oz) oyster mushrooms, thickly sliced
200 g (7 oz) chestnut mushrooms, quartered
1 tablespoon reduced salt soy sauce
1 tablespoon dry sherry
3 tablespoons oyster sauce
1 teaspoon soft light brown sugar
100 ml (3¹/₂ fl oz) hot vegetable stock
1 bunch of spring onions, trimmed and chopped
200 g (7 oz) bean sprouts
300 g (10¹/₂ oz) 'straight to wok' noodles

1   Heat the vegetable oil in a wok or large frying pan and stir fry the chopped garlic for 30 seconds; do not allow it to brown. Add all the mushrooms and stir fry for 1 minute, tossing and mixing well.
2   Add the soy sauce, sherry, oyster sauce, sugar and hot vegetable stock. Reduce the heat slightly and simmer for 4–5 minutes until the mushrooms are just tender.
3   Stir in the spring onions, bean sprouts and noodles. Continue cooking for 2 minutes to warm through the noodles thoroughly. Serve immediately in warm bowls.

SERVES 4
PREPARATION & COOKING TIME: 1 hour
FREEZING: not recommended

BUTTERNUT SQUASH WITH LENTILS & GINGER

The ginger gives a warm flavour to this casserole making it ideal for colder winter days. Butternut squash is a **star amongst vegetables** because it provides lots of beta-carotene and the other antioxidant vitamins, C and E. Serve the casserole on a bed of rice.

PER SERVING: 234 calories, 5 g fat

1 tablespoon vegetable oil
1 onion, sliced
1 garlic clove, crushed
2.5 cm (1 inch) piece of fresh root ginger, peeled and grated
1 butternut squash, peeled, de-seeded and cubed
1 yellow pepper, de-seeded and cubed
$\frac{1}{2}$ teaspoon ground cumin
1 teaspoon ground coriander
150 ml ($\frac{1}{4}$ pint) vegetable stock
400 g can of chopped tomatoes
400 g can of lentils, rinsed and drained
400 g can of cannellini beans, rinsed and drained
freshly ground black pepper
chopped fresh coriander, to garnish

1 Heat the vegetable oil in a large flameproof casserole or a saucepan and gently cook the onions for 4–5 minutes until beginning to soften. Add the crushed garlic and grated ginger and cook for a further 2–3 minutes.

2 Stir in the cubed butternut squash, the yellow pepper, ground cumin and coriander and sauté gently for 5 minutes. Add the vegetable stock and chopped tomatoes and bring up to the boil. Reduce the heat, cover the pan and simmer for 20–25 minutes until the butternut squash is tender.

3 Add the lentils and beans, stir through and continue to cook for a further 5 minutes until the beans are thoroughly warmed through. Season to taste with freshly ground black pepper and serve immediately garnished with chopped fresh coriander.

SERVES 4–6
PREPARATION & COOKING TIME:
45 minutes + 30 minutes cooking
FREEZING: not recommended

PER SERVING: 201 calories, 9 g fat

8 sheets of lasagne
25 g (I oz) reduced fat
Cheddar cheese, grated
I tablespoon grated Parmesan cheese
torn basil leavrs, to garnish

FOR THE TOMATO SAUCE:
I tablespoon olive oil
I onion, chopped finely
2 garlic cloves, crushed
2 x 400 g cans of chopped tomatoes
I tablespoon tomato purée
$\frac{1}{2}$ teaspoon dried basil
$\frac{1}{2}$ teaspoon sugar
150 ml ($\frac{1}{4}$ pint) vegetable stock

FOR THE SPINACH LAYER:
450 g frozen spinach, defrosted
250 g tub of ricotta cheese
$\frac{1}{2}$ teaspoon ground nutmeg
freshly ground black pepper

Tomato, spinach and ricotta are **classic flavourings to accompany pasta** but they are normally used to create cannelloni. This is an easier to assemble version made into a lasagne. You can use ready-to-cook dried sheets of lasagne, but I think the fresh lasagne bought from the chiller cabinet gives a better result. Any left over can be frozen and used another time. Serve with a salad accompaniment.

1   Preheat the oven to Gas Mark 5/electric oven 190°C/fan oven 170°C.
2   To make the tomato sauce, heat the olive oil in a large saucepan and gently cook the onion and garlic until softened. Add the chopped tomatoes, tomato purée, dried basil, sugar and vegetable stock. Bring the mixture up to the boil, cover, then reduce the heat and simmer for 20–25 minutes until the sauce has slightly thickened.
3   Meanwhile, place the defrosted spinach in a sieve and, using the back of a wooden spoon, press against the spinach to remove as much of the excess water as possible. Turn the spinach into a bowl and mix in the ricotta, nutmeg and a good grinding of black pepper.
4   Pour half the tomato sauce over the base of a shallow ovenproof dish, measuring about 20 x 28 cm (8 x 11 inches). Place a layer of four lasagne sheets over the sauce. Spread over the spinach and ricotta mixture, then the last four sheets of lasagne. Cover with the remaining tomato sauce. Sprinkle over the reduced fat Cheddar cheese and the grated Parmesan.
5   Bake in the oven for 25–30 minutes until the cheese on top is melted and lightly browned and the lasagne is heated through. Serve immediately.

TOMATO, SPINACH & RICOTTA LASAGNE

SERVES 4
PREPARATION & COOKING TIME: I hour
FREEZING: not recommended

VEGETABLE KORMA

Kormas, although delicious, are usually made with lots of coconut milk, butter and, sometimes, cream. I have developed this **healthy heart version** using low fat yogurt and a minimum of coconut and ground almonds and yet lost none of the flavour. If you have a mill to grind the desiccated coconut to a finer texture, I find it improves the look of the sauce. This curry has a medium hot spiciness. Serve with freshly boiled basmati rice.

PER SERVING: 363 calories, 22 g fat

I potato, peeled and cut into 2.5 cm (I inch) cubes
2 carrots, cut into 2.5 cm (I inch) chunks
10–12 cauliflower florets
I green pepper, de-seeded and cut into 2.5 cm (I inch) cubes
100 g (3^1/$_2$ oz) peas
100 g (3^1/$_2$ oz) green beans
2 tablespoons vegetable oil
I teaspoon mustard seeds
I onion, sliced
3 garlic cloves, crushed
2.5 cm (I inch) piece of fresh root ginger, peeled and chopped finely
2 tablespoons desiccated coconut
400 g can of chopped tomatoes
400 ml (14 fl oz) low fat plain yogurt
I teaspoon garam masala
I teaspoon ground coriander
I teaspoon ground cumin
^{1}/$_4$–^{1}/$_2$ teaspoon chilli powder
^{1}/$_2$ teaspoon turmeric powder
50 g (1^3/$_4$ oz) ground almonds
salt and freshly ground black pepper
chopped fresh coriander, to garnish

1. Put the potato, carrots and cauliflower in a large saucepan, cover with boiling water and simmer for 5 minutes. Add the green pepper, peas and beans, bring back up to simmering point and cook for a further 3–4 minutes. Drain the vegetables.

2. Heat the oil in a large pan and stir in the mustard seeds. When they start to pop, add the onion, garlic and ginger and cook gently for 5–6 minutes to soften the onion. Stir in the desiccated coconut and cook for a further minute, then add the chopped tomatoes.

3. Meanwhile, mix together the yogurt, spices and ground almonds.

4. Add the vegetables to the onion and tomato mixture. Lower the heat and carefully stir in the spiced yoghurt. Stir to gently combine the sauce with the vegetables and simmer gently for a further 8–10 minutes until the vegetables are completely tender. If you prefer a slightly thinner sauce, stir in up to 100 ml (3^1/$_2$ fl oz) water. Check the seasoning, adding a little salt and plenty of black pepper, if required.

5. Serve the korma with a sprinkling of chopped coriander leaves for garnish.

SERVES 6
PREPARATION & COOKING TIME:
40 minutes + 35 minutes cooking
FREEZING: not recommended

CARROT, CASHEW & CHESTNUT PIE

The **crisp filo pastry** contrasts well with the soft filling in this pie recipe. Interestingly, chestnuts are very low in fat so can still be enjoyed by those who are being careful about their fat intake. Serve the pie hot accompanied by boiled new potatoes and lightly steamed broccoli.

PER SERVING: 527 calories, 27 g fat

3 tablespoons olive oil
I large onion, chopped
2 garlic cloves, chopped
600 g (I lb 5oz) carrots, grated
$^{1}/_{2}$ teaspoon dried marjoram
250 g (9 oz) chestnut mushrooms, sliced
200 g vacuum pack of peeled chestnuts, chopped roughly
200 g (7 oz) cashew nuts, chopped roughly
3 tablespoons chopped fresh flat leaf parsley
3 tablespoons tomato purée
200 g (7 oz) low fat cream cheese
freshly ground black pepper6 large sheets of filo pastry
a little milk for glazing

1 Preheat the oven to Gas Mark 4/electric oven 180°C/fan oven 160°C. Place a circle of non-stick baking parchment in the base of a 20–23 cm (8–9 inch) spring release baking tin, about 8 cm (3$^{1}/_{4}$ inches).

2 Heat 2 tablespoons of the olive oil in a large saucepan. Gently fry the onion and garlic for 4–5 minutes to soften. Add the carrots and marjoram, reduce the heat, cover the pan and sweat the vegetables for 10 minutes, stirring occasionally. Remove from the heat and set aside to cool slightly.

3 Meanwhile, heat the remaining tablespoon of oil in a separate pan and sauté the mushrooms for 3–4 minutes. Add the chopped chestnuts, cashews, parsley and tomato purée along with 2 tablespoons of water. Simmer for a further 2–3 minutes.

4 Stir the cream cheese into the cooled carrots, then combine the carrot mixture with the mushrooms. Season with plenty of freshly ground black pepper.

5 Working quickly so that the filo pastry doesn't dry out, arrange four overlapping sheets of pastry across the base of the prepared tin, easing it into the sides and up over the edge of the tin.

6 Spoon the carrot and nut mixture into the tin and level the top. Cover with the fifth sheet of filo pastry, folding as necessary, then turn down the overhanging pieces of filo. Lightly scrunch up the last sheet of pastry and arrange it attractively over to top of the pie. Brush with a little milk to glaze.

7 Place the pie in the oven and bake for 30 minutes until the pastry is crisp and golden. Leave to rest for a couple of minutes, then open the spring release tin and ease the pie from the base on to a serving plate.

SERVES 4
PREPARATION & COOKING TIME:
15 minutes + 1³/₄ hours cooking
FREEZING: recommended

PORK SPARE RIBS WITH BARBECUE SAUCE & COUSCOUS

Spare ribs make a great supper dish. You need to use your fingers to eat them, so make sure you have lots of paper napkins. Do try the couscous. It makes **a change from rice**, and is much easier and quicker to prepare. It's really important to use a fork to 'fluff up' the couscous before serving. It can be reheated the next day in the microwave.

PER SERVING: 710 calories, 40 g fat

16 pork spare ribs
1 tablespoon sunflower oil
1 onion, chopped finely
1 red pepper, de-seeded and chopped finely
2 garlic cloves, crushed
5 cm (2 inches) fresh ginger, peeled and chopped finely
2 tablespoons tomato purée
1 tablespoon clear honey
1 tablespoon cider vinegar
a good shake of Tabasco sauce
1 wineglass white wine
salt and freshly ground black pepper

FOR THE COUSCOUS:
175 g (6 oz) couscous
350 ml (12 fl oz) boiling water
25 g (1 oz) low fat spread
1 teaspoon ground cumin
pinch of chilli powder

1 Preheat the oven to Gas Mark 6/electric oven 200°C/fan oven 180°C.
2 Put the ribs into a large saucepan, completely cover with water and simmer for 20 minutes. Pour into a colander and leave to drain.
3 Meanwhile, heat the oil and gently fry the onion. Add the pepper and garlic and continue to cook for 2 minutes.
4 Add all the other ingredients and bring to the boil, stirring well. Taste to check the seasoning. It should be sweet, sour and spicy – adjust as necessary.
5 Put the ribs into a shallow roasting tin and pour over the sauce. Cook in the oven for 1¹/₄ hours until tender, browned and crunchy looking.
6 Once the ribs are ready, put the couscous in a large bowl (it will increase in bulk) and pour over the boiling water. Stir well, cover with clingfilm and leave to stand for 3 minutes.
7 Pierce the clingfilm and put into the microwave on High for 2 minutes. Remove the clingfilm, and with a fork 'fluff up' the grains. Stir in the spread, cumin and chilli powder. Pile into a warm dish to serve.

SERVES 6
PREPARATION & COOKING TIME:
20 minutes + 50 minutes cooking
FREEZING: not recommended

PER SERVING: 107 calories, 4 g fat

This dessert is based on a **Victorian nursery pudding**. It's really delicious, very light and so lemony. It is very easy to make, and will impress your friends. The pudding is supposed to be served warm but it is also very good cold the next day.

LEMON PUDDING

3 eggs, separated
50 g (1³/₄ oz) caster sugar
grated zest and juice of
2 lemons (unwaxed if possible)
200 ml (7 fl oz) semi skimmed milk
25 g (1 oz) plain flour
low fat spread for greasing

1 Preheat the oven to Gas Mark 4/electric oven 180°C/fan oven 160°C.
2 Beat together the egg yolks and sugar (an electric whisk is good for this) until thick and creamy. Stir in the lemon zest and juice, milk and flour.

3 In a clean bowl whisk the egg whites until they stand in peaks. Carefully fold the whites into the lemon mixture. Pour into a 1.2 litre (2 pint) greased ovenproof dish. Stand the dish in a roasting tin, and add enough water to come halfway up the sides of the dish. This is called a 'bain marie'.
4 Cook in the oven for 40–50 minutes until golden, well risen, and firm to the touch. Serve warm.

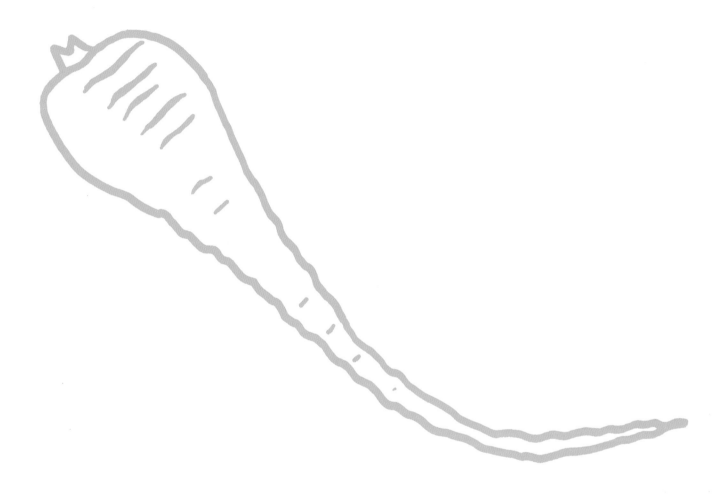

SERVES 4
PREPARATION & COOKING TIME: 20 minutes + 1 hour cooking
FREEZING: recommended

TARRAGON CHICKEN

Fresh tarragon has the most **wonderful aniseed flavour** and goes really well with chicken and fish, but don't ever use dried tarragon – it tastes dreadful. This is traditionally a rich dish, but made with low fat crème fraîche and skinless chicken, it is a good low calorie option. Serve with new potatoes and a green salad.

PER SERVING: 308 calories, 15 g fat

8 chicken thighs, all skin and fat removed
1 wineglass of dry white wine
1/2 onion, sliced finely
25 g (1 oz) fresh tarragon, leaves separated from stalks
1 chicken stock cube
salt and freshly ground black pepper
1/2 x 200 g pot of low fat crème fraîche

1 Preheat the oven to Gas Mark 5/electric oven 190°C/fan oven 170°C.
2 Put the chicken into a flameproof casserole, add the wine, a wineglass of water, the onion, half the tarragon leaves and the tarragon stalks. Crumble over the stock cube, and season with salt and pepper.
3 Cover and cook in the oven for 45 minutes until the chicken is cooked through. Remove the chicken thighs and keep warm. Boil the stock over a high heat until reduced by half, then remove the tarragon stalks.
4 Add the crème fraîche (don't worry if it looks curdled) and boil, stirring well until the sauce thickens. Add the remaining tarragon leaves, lightly chopped, and taste to check the seasoning.
5 Put the chicken back into the sauce, stir well and serve.

SERVES 4
PREPARATION & COOKING TIME: 25 minutes
FREEZING: not recommended

CHINESE STYLE CHICKEN

The secret of a good stir fry is having all of the **ingredients prepared beforehand**. The actual cooking is simple and very quick.

PER SERVING: 136 calories, 5 g fat

2 chicken breasts, skinned and sliced into thin strips
2 teaspoons Chinese five spice powder
1 tablespoon sesame oil
1 garlic clove, sliced finely
a walnut-sized piece of fresh ginger, peeled, sliced and cut into matchsticks
1 bunch of spring onions, trimmed and sliced diagonally
100 g (3 1/2 oz) mange tout, trimmed and halved
1 green pepper, halved, de-seeded and sliced finely
a good shake of light soy sauce

1 Toss the chicken strips in the five spice powder.
2 Heat the oil in a non-stick wok, add the garlic and ginger and quickly fry until just golden. Add the chicken and fry for 3–4 minutes.
3 Remove the chicken, garlic and ginger and keep warm. Add all the prepared vegetables to the wok together with 3 tablespoons of water.
4 Stir fry over a high heat for 2 minutes until the water has evaporated. Return the chicken, garlic and ginger to the pan. Add soy sauce and toss to mix well. Serve immediately.

SERVES 4
PREPARATION & COOKING TIME: I hour marinating + 40 minutes
FREEZING: not recommended

SERVES 4
PREPARATION & COOKING TIME: 25 minutes
FREEZING: not recommended

COLD SPICY BEEF FILLET

These steaks could be **cooked on the barbecue**. Three minutes per side will give you medium rare – adjust the cooking times to suit your tastes. Bulgar wheat is similar to couscous but with a coarser and nuttier texture.

PER SERVING: 276 calories, 9 g fat

I teaspoon whole coriander seeds
I garlic clove
salt and freshly ground black pepper
$^{1}/_{2}$ small onion, grated
juice of $^{1}/_{2}$ lemon
I tablespoon olive oil
2 x 150 g (5$^{1}/_{2}$ oz) beef fillet steaks
125 g (4$^{1}/_{2}$ oz) bulgar wheat
600 ml (I pint) boiling water
125 g (4$^{1}/_{2}$ oz) white grapes, halved and de-seeded
2 tablespoons French dressing (page 00)
2 tablespoons chopped fresh parsley

1 Using a pestle and mortar, crush the coriander seeds, garlic, salt and pepper to a paste. Add the grated onion, lemon juice and oil.
2 Spread this mixture on to both sides of the steaks, cover and leave to marinate in the fridge for I hour.
3 Meanwhile, soak the bulgar wheat in the boiling water for 30 minutes.
4 Using a non-stick frying pan, fry the steaks (and any marinade) for 3 minutes on each side. Let the steaks rest for 5 minutes before slicing into thin strips.
5 Drain the bulgar wheat and put in a large serving bowl with the grapes and French dressing. Mix well.
6 Top the salad with the beef, and sprinkle with chopped parsley to serve.

ORIENTAL BEEF

This is a delicious, different and **easy way to cook** fillet steak. It's very good served with noodles and a green salad.

PER SERVING: 195 calories, 13 g fat

I small fresh green chilli, halved and de-seeded (optional)
I lemon grass stalk, bruised
I chicken stock cube
4 thin slices of fresh ginger
I garlic clove, crushed
2 x 175 g (6 oz) fillet steaks, trimmed of all fat
2 tablespoons sesame oil
cooked Chinese noodles, to serve

1 Put the chilli, lemon grass, stock cube, ginger, garlic and 300 ml ($^{1}/_{2}$ pint) water in a frying pan. Bring to the boil, stirring well to melt the stock cube.
2 Pop in the steaks, making sure they are completely covered with the stock. Poach in barely simmering stock for 4 minutes (for medium rare).
3 Remove the steaks and keep warm, resting on kitchen towel. Boil the stock to reduce to about 4 tablespoons. With a slotted spoon remove the flavourings and stir in the oil.
4 Thinly slice the steaks, arrange on top of the noodles and pour the sauce over.

We all deserve rewards, and you are more likely to continue eating a low calorie diet if you allow yourself an occasional treat. The crisp Oat & Cinnamon Biscuits are good to accompany fruit puddings, and are ideal served after dinner with coffee.

Most of the puddings are fruit based, which is both the healthiest and the most delicious way to end a low calorie

PUDDINGS & TREATS

meal. The Pink Grapefruit & Vodka Sorbet is wonderfully refreshing and a great palate cleanser too. Do try the Lemon Pudding – it's so comforting.

Why should people watching their calorie intake be denied home made scones? Using half fat crème fraîche and fresh raspberries makes them a viable choice, and a real treat.

MAKES 12
PREPARATION & COOKING TIME:
15 minutes + 15 minutes cooking
FREEZING: not recommended

These little biscuits do contain fat, but only 50 g (1³/₄ oz) for 12 biscuits. The oats and ground rice give them a **lovely texture**. Serve with puddings, as a treat, or with after dinner coffee.

OAT & CINNAMON BISCUITS

PER SERVING: 67 calories, 2 g fat

50 g (1³/₄ oz) self raising flour
50 g (1³/₄ oz) ground rice
50 g (1³/₄ oz) porridge oats
25 g (1 oz) soft brown sugar
1 teaspoon ground cinnamon
grated zest of 1 orange
65 g (2¹/₄ oz) low fat spread plus extra for greasing

1 Preheat the oven to Gas Mark 6/electric oven 200°C/fan oven 180°C.
2 Mix all the dry ingredients and orange rind together in a large bowl.
3 Melt the low fat spread, cool, then pour on to the flour mixture. With a wooden spoon bring together to form a ball.

4 Divide the dough into 12, and roll into small balls. Put on a greased baking sheet and press down on each one with the back of a fork.
5 Cook in the oven for 12–15 minutes until golden. Cool on a wire rack. The biscuits can be stored 3–4 days in an airtight tin.

SERVES 4
PREPARATION TIME: 20 minutes
FREEZING: not recommended

PER SERVING: 65 calories, 0 g fat

This is a very pretty and simple fruit salad using fruits available in the autumn. The pomegranate is sweet and pink, and adds **an unusual flavour**. Put a little honey with the orange juice if you have a sweet tooth.

AUTUMN FRUIT SALAD

2 Williams, Comice or Conference pears
2 Russet apples
juice of ¹/₂ orange
a little clear honey (optional)
I pomegranate

1   Peel the pears and cut into quarters. Remove the core and slice into a serving dish. Leave the apples unpeeled. Cut them into quarters, remove the core and slice into the dish.

2   Pour over the orange juice and honey, if used, and turn to mix. This prevents the fruit from going brown.

3   Cut the pomegranate in half over a large dinner plate (to save all the juices). With a teaspoon handle or a fork, ease out the pink seeds, making sure to remove all the membranes as these can be bitter.

4   Add the pomegranate seeds and all their juices to the other fruit. Stir to mix and serve alone or with oat & cinnamon biscuits (page 68).

SERVES 4
PREPARATION TIME:
10 minutes + 2 hours freezing
FREEZING: essential

PER SERVING: 135 calories, 0 g fat

425 ml (³/₄ pint) pink grapefruit juice
75 g (2³/₄ oz) caster sugar
3 tablespoons vodka or gin

This sorbet **looks very pretty** and has a wonderful palate-cleansing taste. It can be made by hand, but an ice cream machine is an excellent investment.

1 Heat a little of the grapefruit juice with the sugar in a small saucepan until the sugar has dissolved. Remove from the heat and stir in the remaining grapefruit juice together with the vodka or gin.

2 If using an ice cream machine follow the manufacturer's instructions. Otherwise, pour into a suitable plastic container and freeze until ice crystals form around the edges. Beat well and return to the freezer.

3 Repeat this two or three times until the sorbet is thick, smooth and well frozen. It should not contain any large lumps of ice.

4 Allow to 'soften' in the fridge for about 15 minutes before freezing.

PINK GRAPEFRUIT & VODKA SORBET

SERVES 6
PREPARATION & COOKING TIME: 30 minutes + 2 hours setting
FREEZING: not recommended

SILKEN TOFU COFFEE CHEESECAKE

Silken tofu, available from health food shops, makes an **excellent smooth cheesecake**. It's a good alternative to calorie-rich cream cheese. Don't be nervous of gelatine: as long as it is not overheated or added to a very cold mixture, it is easy to use. Low fat crème fraîche would be a good accompaniment.

PER SERVING: 213 calories, 9 g fat

12 ginger nut biscuits
25 g (1 oz) low fat spread
3 teaspoons good quality instant coffee granules
1 sachet powdered gelatine
300 g (10½ oz) silken tofu
1 tablespoon clear honey
a small bunch of black grapes, halved and de-seeded, to decorate

1   Crush the biscuits in a food processor. Melt the spread in a saucepan over a low heat. Add the crushed biscuits and mix well. Press into the bottom of a 20 cm (8 inch) shallow dish (or foil tray) and leave to set.
2   Meanwhile, put 150 ml (¼ pint) cold water and the coffee in a small saucepan, and sprinkle over the gelatine. Set over a low heat and stir with a wooden spoon until the gelatine has dissolved and the liquid is clear. Be careful not to overheat. Leave to cool for 5 minutes.
3   Rinse out the processor, add the tofu and honey, and pulse to mix. With the motor running, pour in the cooled coffee and gelatine until mixed well.
4   Quickly pour the tofu mixture over the biscuit base. Put in the fridge to set for about 2 hours. Decorate with the grapes to serve.

SERVES 4
PREPARATION & COOKING TIME: 35 minutes + 3 hours chilling
FREEZING: not recommended

CITRUS FRUIT SALAD

This very refreshing fruit salad is a **speciality of the Alicante region** in Spain. Oranges and almonds grow profusely within the province and keeping bees is popular too. If you can't find any orange flower water, just use ordinary water.

PER SERVING: 305 calories, 18 g fat

2 tablespoons clear honey (more if you have a sweet tooth)
2 tablespoons orange flower water
4 Spanish oranges, peeled and all white pith removed
I pink grapefruit, peeled and all white pith removed
125 g (4½ oz) flaked almonds

1 Mix together the honey and orange flower water. Thinly slice the oranges and grapefruit over a dish to reserve the juice. Remove any pips.
2 Layer the fruit in a pretty glass bowl, sprinkling the honey mixture over as you go. Cover and leave for at least 3 hours in the fridge.
3 Meanwhile, brown the almonds, either under the grill or in the oven, being careful not to burn them.
4 Sprinkle the almonds over the fruit to serve.

SERVES 4
PREPARATION & COOKING TIME:
30 minutes + 20 minutes cooling
FREEZING: not recommended

PINK RHUBARB FOOL

Forced or Champagne rhubarb, the **beautiful pink spears** that are in the shops in early spring, is best for this recipe. You can use other types of rhubarb available throughout the year. Just add a little more honey, and you might need to remove the tough outer skin as well.

PER SERVING: 75 calories, 0 g fat

450 g (1 lb) forced rhubarb, leaves removed and stalks trimmed
I tablespoon clear honey
juice of I orange
250 g tub of virtually fat free Quark
oat & cinnamon biscuits (page 68), to serve

1 Preheat the oven to Gas Mark 5/electric oven 190°C/fan oven 170°C.
2 Chop the rhubarb into chunks and put in an ovenproof dish with the honey and orange juice.
3 Cook in the oven for 15–20 minutes until the rhubarb is soft. It will make its own juice. Leave to cool.
4 Put the cooled rhubarb and all the juices in a food processor. Add the Quark and pulse gently to mix. Pile into a serving dish and serve with oat & cinnamon biscuits.

MAKES 6 medium or 12 small scones
PREPARATION & COOKING TIME:
15 minutes + 15 minutes cooking
FREEZING: recommended

PER SMALL SCONE: 119 calories,
5 g fat

Scones are **easy to make at home**, and are so much nicer than the shop-bought ones. They freeze well too. You can take one or two out of the freezer, microwave for 10–15 seconds, and they will then be warm and ready to receive the fruit and crème fraîche. If you have milk that has turned sour, use this to make the scones.

225 g (8 oz) plain flour plus extra for dusting
1 heaped teaspoon baking powder
25 g (1 oz) butter
150 ml (¼ pint) semi skimmed milk

TO SERVE:
175 g (6 oz) fresh raspberries or blueberries
200 g pot of half fat crème fraîche

1 Preheat the oven to Gas Mark 7/electric oven 220°C/fan oven 200°C.
2 Sieve the flour and baking powder into a large bowl and rub in the butter using just your fingertips.
3 Using one hand, add enough milk to make a soft but not sticky dough, Turn on to a floured surface and knead lightly. Roll out to 2.5 cm (1 inch) thick.
4 Cut into circles with a cutter (whatever size you choose) and put on to a floured baking sheet.
5 Cook in the oven for 15–20 minutes until well risen and golden. Place on a wire rack and serve warm or cold with the crème fraîche and fruit.

SCONES WITH CRÈME FRAÎCHE & RASPBERRIES

SERVES 4
PREPARATION & COOKING TIME:
1 hour + 1 hour cooling
FREEZING: not recommended

PER SERVING: 215 calories, 7 g fat

Victoria plums are the best, available from August to September, but other varieties are almost as good. This can be **prepared the day before** and left in the fridge.

POACHED PLUMS

1 wineglass fruity red wine
75 g (2³/₄ oz) golden granulated sugar
500 g (1 lb 2 oz) plums
50 g (1³/₄ oz) flaked almonds,
lightly browned under the grill

1 Add enough water to the wine to make it up to 600 ml (1 pint). Put the liquid and sugar into a large saucepan, bring to the boil and simmer for 2 minutes.
2 Put in the plums one by one with a slotted spoon. They need to be in a single layer and completely covered with the liquid.

3 Bring back to the boil, cover, and simmer for 3–4 minutes for Victoria plums and a little longer for larger harder varieties. Turn off the heat and leave the plums in the juice (still covered) for 30 minutes.
4 Remove the plums with a slotted spoon. Boil the juice to reduce by half, pour over the plums and leave to cool for at least an hour, and preferably overnight. Serve cold in a pretty glass bowl with the almonds sprinkled over at the last moment. Serve alone or with a low fat crème fraîche.

Those who love their puddings and desserts will be glad to know that they are not forbidden in a healthy heart diet! Once again, it's a case of thinking wisely about what you are going to eat.

Fruit, of course, features highly in the list of what to have and there are some totally delicious recipes in this chapter solely based on fruit. Why not try the Tropical Fruit Salad with a Lime & Ginger Syrup or the Roasted Spiced Fruit Bowls? Apart from being scrumptious they will contribute to the five fruit and vegetable per day tally, as well as providing those essential antioxidants and vitamins. Traditional

PUDDINGS & DESSERTS

puddings, like crumbles, are often high in saturated fats, but they can also be enjoyed by using an unsaturated margarine instead of butter and including some good-for-you oats, nuts or seeds in with the flour for the topping.

There is now an increasing range of low fat dairy items, such as fromage frais, Quark, low fat Greek yogurt and crème fraîche, that can be served with puddings or used as the base for mousses and fruit fools. So, leave behind the creamy custards and dollops of clotted cream and move forward into low fat dairy choices or even fruit sauces to accompany your puds!

SERVES 4–6
PREPARATION & COOKING TIME: 20 minutes + 2 hours setting
FREEZING: not recommended

CHOCOLATE MOCHA MOUSSE

Eating healthily doesn't mean cutting out chocolate completely, but it does mean keeping it **as a treat** for every now and again. Plain dark chocolate (and the higher the cocoa solids, the better) contains useful antioxidants, iron and less fat than milk chocolate. This mousse recipe also uses virtually fat free Quark instead of double cream.

PER SERVING: 189 calories, 10 g fat

100 g (3¹/₂ oz) plain chocolate, 70% cocoa solids
2 tablespoons strong coffee
3 eggs, separated
250 g tub of Quark, at room temperature
25 g (1 oz) caster sugar
chocolate curls, to decorate

1 Melt the chocolate in a small bowl over a pan of hot water. Stir in the coffee and the egg yolks and mix well. Set aside to cool slightly.
2 In a large bowl, whisk the egg whites until they are stiff but not dry.
3 Place the Quark in a bowl and stir until smooth, adding in the caster sugar. Carefully stir in the chocolate mixture until well combined. It's important that the Quark is almost at room temperature because if it is used straight from the fridge its coldness will cause the chocolate to 'set' and they will not combine smoothly.
4 Stir one spoonful of the egg white into the mixture to loosen it up, then carefully fold in the rest taking care not to knock out the volume.
5 Divide the mousse between 4–6 ramekin dishes or coffee cups and place in the fridge for about 1¹/₂–2 hours to set. Decorate each mousse with a few chocolate curls before serving.

SERVES 4–6
PREPARATION & COOKING TIME:
20 minutes + 12 minutes cooking + 1 hour chilling
FREEZING: not recommended

TROPICAL FRUIT SALAD WITH A LIME & GINGER SYRUP

A refreshing fruit salad with a difference. The stem ginger provides a subtle background warmth to the syrup and the tropical fruits supply **a wealth of vitamins**. Chill the fruit salad only very lightly before serving – if you allow it to become too cold, the subtle flavours will be lost completely.

PER SERVING: 129 calories, 0 g fat

FOR THE SYRUP:
50 g (1³/₄ oz) caster sugar
grated zest and juice of 1 lime
1 tablespoon stem ginger syrup

FOR THE FRUIT SALAD:
1 small sweet pineapple
1 large ripe mango
2 kiwi fruit
1 ripe pawpaw
2 pieces of stem ginger, chopped finely

1   To make the syrup, place the caster sugar in a small pan with 200 ml (7 fl oz) water. Dissolve the sugar over a low heat, stirring occasionally, and then add the lime zest. Bring to the boil and simmer gently for 10 minutes to form a sugar syrup. Remove from the heat and stir in the lime juice and the stem ginger syrup. Set aside to cool.

2   Meanwhile, peel and cube the pineapple and mango. Peel and slice the kiwi fruit. Halve the pawpaw, remove the seeds, peel and slice. Place the prepared fruit and the finely chopped stem ginger in a large glass serving dish and pour over the cooled syrup. Carefully turn the fruit in the syrup. Place the fruit salad in the fridge for an hour before serving to chill lightly and allow the flavours to blend.

SERVES 6
PREPARATION & COOKING TIME:
25 minutes + 35 minutes cooking
FREEZING: recommended

HARVEST FRUIT CRUMBLE

Fruit crumbles are one of the most popular desserts ever but if butter is used the topping can be high in saturated fat. Substituting a polyunsaturated margarine, as well as using **oats and walnuts in the crumble**, is a much healthier option. Serve with some low fat custard to pour over.

PER SERVING: 446 calories, 21 g fat

2 Bramley apples, peeled, cored and sliced
2 pears, peeled, cored and sliced
3 plums, stoned and sliced
75 g (2³/₄ oz) soft light brown sugar
¹/₂ teaspoon ground cinnamon

FOR THE CRUMBLE:
150 g (5¹/₂ oz) plain flour
75 g (2³/₄ oz) rolled oats
100 g (3¹/₂ oz) sunflower margarine
50 g (1³/₄ oz) walnuts, chopped roughly
¹/₂ teaspoon ground cinnamon
75 g (2³/₄ oz) demerara sugar

1   Preheat the oven to Gas Mark 4/electric oven 180°C/fan oven 160°C.

2   Place the prepared fruit, the light brown sugar and the cinnamon in an ovenproof dish. Stir lightly to combine and ensure the sugar coats the fruit.

3   Put the plain flour and oats in a mixing bowl and rub in the margarine. Stir in the walnuts, cinnamon and demerara sugar and mix well. Spoon the crumble topping evenly over the fruit.

4   Bake the crumble in the oven for 30–35 minutes until the fruit is tender and the topping crisp and lightly golden.

SERVES 8
PREPARATION & COOKING TIME:
40 minutes + 30 minutes cooking
FREEZING: not recommended

PER SERVING: 181 calories, 3 g fat

Roulades make an **elegant dessert for a dinner party** and are not as difficult to make as you may think. Filled with low fat Greek yogurt and served with a fruit sauce instead of pouring cream, this is a delicious low fat version. In the winter, when strawberries are not so flavoursome, a large ripe mango could be used as a substitute.

1 Preheat the oven to Gas Mark 2/electric oven 150°C/fan oven 130°C. Line a 33 × 23 cm (13 × 9 inch) Swiss roll tin with non-stick baking parchment.
2 Place the egg whites in a large bowl and beat with an electric whisk until stiff but not dry. Gradually whisk in the caster sugar until the mixture is thick and shiny and meringue-like. Finally, whisk in the cornflour, vinegar, vanilla extract and the grated orange zest.
3 Transfer the meringue mixture to the prepared tin, spread it out and level gently. Place in the oven and bake for 25–30 minutes until the surface of the meringue is golden and just firm.
4 Remove the meringue from the oven and cover with a clean, damp tea towel for 10 minutes.
5 Place a length of non-stick baking parchment, larger than the area of the meringue, on the work surface. Turn the roulade out of the tin and on to the baking parchment. Spread the yogurt over the meringue, then scatter over half the sliced strawberries. Use the edge of the paper to help roll up the meringue into a roulade and place on the serving dish.
6 Liquidise the remaining strawberries with the orange juice and then pass through a sieve to remove the seeds. If necessary, stir in 1–2 tablespoons of icing sugar to sweeten the fruit sauce. Serve the roulade in slices, accompanied by the strawberry sauce.

3 large egg whites
175 g (6 oz) caster sugar
1 level teaspoon cornflour
1 teaspoon malt vinegar
1 teaspoon vanilla extract
grated zest and juice of 1 large orange
400 g (14 oz) ripe strawberries, hulled and sliced
500 g pot of low fat Greek yogurt
1–2 tablespoons icing sugar

STRAWBERRY & ORANGE MERINGUE ROULADE WITH FRESH STRAWBERRY SAUCE

SERVES 4
PREPARATION & COOKING TIME:
25 minutes + 25 minutes cooking
FREEZING: not recommended

ROASTED SPICED FRUIT BOWLS

Roasting fruit has become a very popular way of serving it for dessert, but it usually involves lots of butter. This delicious recipe **does not use butter** and is just as flavoursome. If you do not like the seeds of passion fruit, then rub the fruit through a sieve and simply drizzle the pulp over the roasted fruit. If you feel the dessert needs an accompaniment, serve with a bowl of low fat Greek yogurt to spoon over the fruit.

PER SERVING: 215 calories, 1 g fat

1 small pineapple, peeled, cored, quartered and cut into bite size wedges
2 large bananas, cut into chunks
1 large mango, peeled, stoned and cubed
2 tablespoons golden syrup
1 teaspoon ground cinnamon
a generous pinch of nutmeg
3 tablespoons soft light brown sugar
zest and juice of 1 orange
2 ripe passion fruit

1 Preheat the oven to Gas Mark 6/electric oven 200°C/fan oven 180°C. Cut four 30 cm (12 inch) squares of foil.
2 Divide the pieces of prepared pineapple, banana and mango equally between the sheets of foil, placing them in the centre. Scrunch up the edges of the foil around the fruit to form open 'bowls'. Place the bowls on baking sheets.
3 Put the golden syrup, cinnamon, nutmeg, brown sugar and orange zest and juice in a small pan and heat gently until melted and combined together. Pour the syrup equally over the fruit.
4 Roast the fruit in the oven for 20–25 minutes until the fruit is tender and just beginning to brown.
5 Halve the passion fruit and scoop out the flesh. Spoon over the roasted fruit and serve immediately, leaving the fruit in its 'bowl' if desired.

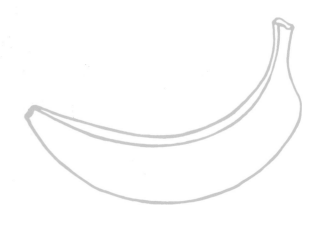

SERVES 4
PREPARATION & COOKING TIME: 30 minutes + I hour chilling
FREEZING: not recommended

APPLE, APRICOT & AMARETTI LAYER DESSERT

Plenty of soluble fibre is found in this dessert, but don't over process the fruit into too smooth a purée because it is nice to have some **texture from the apricots**. This dessert layers up very attractively in glass tumblers.

PER SERVING: 368 calories, 7 g fat

500 g (I lb 2 oz) apples, peeled, cored and sliced
225 g (8 oz) no need to soak apricots, chopped roughly
2 tablespoons amaretto liqueur
125 g (4 1/2 oz) amaretti biscuits, crushed
250 g (9 oz) fromage frais.

1 Place the apples and apricots in a pan and add 100 ml (3 1/2 fl oz) water. Cook gently until the apples are pulpy and the apricots have softened. Allow to cool and then place in a food processor and process to a rough purée. Stir in the amaretto liqueur.
2 Put a layer of crushed amaretti biscuits in the base of each of four glasses. Using half of the fruit purée, put an equal layer in each glass.
3 Reserve 4 dessertspoons of the fromage frais, then divide the rest equally between the glasses.
4 Reserve I tablespoon of the crushed biscuits and layer the rest equally over the fromage frais. Divide the fruit purée between the glasses to create the last layer.
5 Place a dessertspoon of the reserved fromage frais in the centre of each and sprinkle with the last of the crushed biscuits. Chill the dessert for an hour before serving.

SERVES 4
PREPARATION & COOKING TIME:
20 minutes + 20 minutes cooking
FREEZING: not recommended

DATE, RAISIN & GINGER STUFFED BAKED APPLES

Apples with their soluble fibre can help to lower cholesterol and, because of their low glycaemic count, they provide slow release energy, which should prevent us from feeling hungry and snacking. Again, a traditional style dessert, but with a **delicious stuffing**. Do ensure that you have removed all the rough core and that there is sufficient space in the centre of the apples to pack in the stuffing. Serve with some low fat custard to pour over.

PER SERVING: 282 calories, 9 g fat

4 cooking apples, cored
75 g (2 3/4 oz) dates, chopped
50 g (1 3/4 oz) raisins
50 g (1 3/4 oz) pecan nuts, chopped finely
2 pieces of stem ginger, chopped finely
I tablespoon stem ginger syrup
I tablespoon clear honey

1 Preheat the oven to Gas Mark 4/electric oven 180°C/fan oven 160°C. Line a baking tin with a sheet of non-stick baking parchment.
2 Score the apples lightly around the middle and place in the baking tin.
3 Mix together the dates, raisins, pecans and chopped stem ginger. Pack equal amounts into the centre of the apples, pushing down well.
4 Stir together the stem ginger syrup and the honey and spoon it over the dried fruit filling, allowing it to drizzle down inside the apples and slightly over the surface.
5 Place the apples in the oven and bake for 20 minutes or until the apples feel soft when the sides are pressed gently. Serve warm.

SERVES 8
PREPARATION & COOKING TIME:
1¼ hours + 2 hours setting
FREEZING: not recommended

PER SERVING: 191 calories, 2 g fat

Strawberry and lime combine to make a **wonderfully refreshing flavour** to this cheesecake as well as providing plenty of vitamin C. Again, using Quark and very low fat Greek yogurt makes this another 'healthy option' dessert.

1 Preheat the oven to Gas Mark 4/electric oven 180°C/fan oven 160°C. Lightly grease and line with greaseproof paper the base of a 20 cm (8 inch) loose bottomed cake tin or spring release tin.

2 To make the sponge, break the eggs into a large bowl and add the caster sugar. Whisk with an electric hand mixer until the mixture is thick, light in colour and creamy. When the whisk is lifted out of the mixture, a trail should be left across the surface.

3 Sift the flour on to the surface of the whisked mixture and fold in carefully, using a large metal spoon. Turn the mixture into the prepared cake tin and spread out evenly. Bake in the oven for 20–25 minutes until the sponge is risen, lightly golden and just beginning to shrink from the sides of the cake tin. Turn out and leave to cool on a wire rack.

4 Wash out the cake tin, dry, and line the sides and base with greaseproof paper.

5 For the filling, place the Quark and Greek yogurt in a large bowl and stir in the caster sugar and the lime zest. Pour the lime juice into a small bowl and sprinkle over the gelatine powder. Leave for 5 minutes to 'sponge', then stand the bowl over a pan of gently simmering water until the gelatine granules have dissolved completely. Set it aside to cool slightly.

6 Using a sharp knife, carefully split the cold cake in half horizontally and place the base back in the tin, cut side up. Thinly slice five or six equal sized strawberries lengthways and place the slices around the edge of the cake tin. Reserve at least four strawberries for decoration and finely chop the rest. Stir the chopped strawberries and the cooled gelatine into the cheese mixture and stir to combine well.

7 Carefully spoon the cheesecake mixture into the tin, taking care not to knock over any of the strawberry slices around the edge. Level the surface of the cheese mixture and place the remaining sponge layer on top with the cut side down on to the cheese. Cover the tin with clingfilm and leave in the fridge for 1½–2 hours to set.

8 To serve, remove from the cake tin and carefully peel off the greaseproof paper. Transfer to a serving plate, dust the top with icing sugar and decorate with the reserved strawberries.

FOR THE SPONGE:
2 eggs
75 g (2¾ oz) caster sugar
50 g (1¼ oz) self raising flour
icing sugar for dusting

FOR THE FILLING:
2 x 250 g cartons of Quark
150 g pot of no fat Greek yogurt
75 g (2¾ oz) caster sugar
zest and juice of 2 limes
1 sachet of gelatine powder
400 g (14 oz) fresh strawberries, hulled

STRAWBERRY & LIME ANGEL CHEESECAKE

There is nothing quite like the aroma of freshly baked bread and cakes wafting through the house, and the best thing about baking your own is that you know exactly what goes into them. Commercially produced cakes are usually high in fat (trans-fatty acids, at that), loaded with sugar and laced with preservatives.

On the other hand, if you make your own using the recipes in this chapter, you can create fatless sponges, healthy flapjack-style bars, muffins made with sunflower oil instead of butter and delicious fruit loaves. Instead of using only white flour, some of the recipes use wholemeal or half and half of each, to provide some extra essential fibre and some of those B group vitamins.

CAKES & BAKING

Adding seeds, such as sesame or sunflower, to breads and cakes will also increase our intake of the essential fatty acids we need, as well as providing a good source of minerals.

Special occasions like birthdays demand a special cake, and the Chocolate Orange Celebration Gateau will not disappoint. The fat content has been kept as low as possible by using a whisked sponge for the cake and making the filling from no fat Greek yoghurt. So, don't feel guilty when you fill the cake tin. As long as you are using the best possible options for healthy heart eating, indulging every now and again in a slice of home made cake is a treat worth enjoying.

MAKES 12 SLICES
PREPARATION & COOKING TIME:
20 minutes + 50 minutes cooking
FREEZING: not recommended

MAKES 12–14 SLICES
PREPARATION & COOKING TIME:
10 minutes + overnight soaking + 1¼ hours cooking
FREEZING: recommended

BANANA, APRICOT & WALNUT CAKE

SPICED ORANGE TEABREAD

A **delicious moist loaf-type cake** which is good in lunchboxes or for picnics. Make sure the bananas are really ripe when you use them to allow their flavour to come through in the cake.

PER SERVING: 237 calories, 13 g fat

100 g (3½ oz) sunflower margarine plus extra for greasing
100 g (3½ oz) soft light brown sugar
2 eggs, beaten lightly
75 g (2¾ oz) walnuts, chopped roughly
50g (1¾ oz) ready to eat dried apricots, chopped roughly
2 bananas, mashed
½ teaspoon mixed spice
225 g (8 oz) self raising white flour

1 Preheat the oven to Gas Mark 4/electric oven 180°C/fan oven 160°C. Grease a 900 g (2 lb) loaf tin with sunflower margarine and line the base with greaseproof paper.
2 Cream the margarine and sugar until light and fluffy, then gradually beat in the eggs.
3 Reserve a quarter of the chopped walnuts then fold the rest into the creamed mixture along with the apricots and mashed bananas.
4 Fold in the mixed spice and flour. Transfer the mixture to the prepared tin, level the surface and sprinkle over the reserved walnuts.
5 Bake in the oven for 45–50 minutes until risen, golden and firm to the touch. A skewer inserted into the middle of the cake should come out clean.
6 Allow to cool in the tin for 5 minutes then turn out on to a wire rack to complete cooling. Cut into slices for serving.

This is a lovely moist teabread, full of flavour and low in fat. The flavour actually **improves on keeping**, but wrap it in foil to keep it from drying out.

PER SERVING: 192 calories, 1 g fat

150 g (5½ oz) sultanas
150 g (5½ oz) raisins
50 g (1¾ oz) mixed chopped peel
grated zest and juice of 1 orange
175 g (6 oz) soft light brown sugar
approximately 200 ml (7 fl oz) hot strong tea
300 g (10½ oz) self raising wholemeal flour
1 teaspoon mixed spice
1 egg, lightly beaten
a little vegetable oil for greasing

1 Place the dried fruit, grated orange zest and sugar into a medium sized bowl. Pour the orange juice into a measuring jug and add sufficient tea to make 300 ml (½ pint) of liquid. Pour this over the fruit and stir well to dissolve the sugar. Cover the bowl and leave overnight to allow the fruit to swell.
2 Preheat the oven to Gas Mark 2/electric oven 150°C/fan oven 130°C. Grease a 900 g (2 lb) loaf tin and line the base with greaseproof paper.
3 Stir the flour, mixed spice and beaten egg into the fruit mixture. Mix thoroughly, then transfer into the loaf tin and level the surface.
4 Bake in the oven for about 1–1¼ hours until risen and firm to the touch. A fine skewer inserted into the middle of the loaf should come out clean. Leave to cool in the tin for 10 minutes, then turn out on to a wire rack to cool completely. Cut into slices for serving and spread thinly with a polyunsaturated margarine.

MAKES 12 SQUARES
PREPARATION & COOKING TIME:
25 minutes + 35 minutes cooking
FREEZING: recommended

PASSION CAKE SQUARES

Passion cake or, to give it its more ordinary name, carrot cake is one of those cakes which seem to be very indulgent but actually is fairly healthy. With vegetable oil instead of butter in the cake mix and Quark for the topping, then **plenty of fibre, vitamins and minerals** from the fruit, wholemeal flour and nuts, the whole thing is not quite as naughty as it sounds.

PER SERVING: 408 calories, 25 g fat

125 g (4$\frac{1}{2}$ oz) self raising white flour
125 g (4$\frac{1}{2}$ oz) self raising wholemeal flour
2 teaspoons baking powder
1 teaspoon ground mixed spice
$\frac{1}{2}$ teaspoon ground nutmeg
125 g (4$\frac{1}{2}$ oz) soft light brown sugar
150 g (5$\frac{1}{2}$ oz) carrots, grated
grated zest and juice of 1 orange
50 g (1$\frac{3}{4}$ oz) pecan nuts, chopped roughly, plus 12, to decorate
200 ml (7 fl oz) sunflower oil plus extra for greasing
2 eggs, beaten lightly
2 ripe bananas, mashed

FOR THE TOPPING:
250 g tub of Quark
75 g (2$\frac{3}{4}$ oz) icing sugar, sieved
2 teaspoons orange juice

1 Preheat the oven to Gas Mark 4/electric oven 180°C/fan oven 160°C. Grease a 28 x 19 cm (11 x 7$\frac{1}{2}$ inch) baking tin with sunflower oil and line the base with greaseproof paper.
2 Place all the ingredients for the cake in a large mixing bowl and beat well until thoroughly combined. Transfer the mixture into the prepared baking tin and bake in the oven for 30–35 minutes until firm on the top and a skewer inserted in the middle comes out clean.
3 Remove the cake from the tin, peel off the greaseproof paper and leave to cool on a wire rack.
4 To make the topping, put the Quark, icing sugar and orange juice into a bowl and mix well together until smooth and creamy. Spread evenly over the top of the cake and swirl with a knife to create an interesting effect. Cut the cake into 12 squares and place a pecan nut in the centre of each square.
5 The cake will keep for several days in an airtight container in the fridge.

SERVES 8–12
PREPARATION & COOKING TIME:
1 hour
FREEZING: not recommended

PER SERVING: 208 calories, 10 g fat

At birthdays or celebration times it is easy to forget healthy eating guidelines and become rather carried away with the event. This gateau, however, does everything possible to minimise the damage yet still **tastes rich and scrumptious!** It is based on a fat free whisked sponge and uses lower fat ricotta cheese instead of double cream for filling and topping.

4 eggs
125 g (4¹/₂ oz) caster sugar
100 g (3¹/₂ oz) self raising white flour
25 g (1 oz) cocoa powder
¹/₂ teaspoon baking powder
¹/₂ teaspoon vanilla extract
grated zest of 1 orange
a little vegetable oil for greasing
1 orange, to decorate (optional)

FOR THE FILLING:
1 orange
200g (7 oz) no fat yogurt
2 tablespoons reduced sugar orange marmalade

FOR THE TOPPING:
100 g (3¹/₂ oz) packet plain chocolate, 70% cocoa solids
45 g (¹/₂ oz) butter
2 tablespoons caster sugar

1 Preheat the oven to Gas Mark 4/electric oven 180°C/fan oven 160°C. Lightly grease and line the base of two 20 cm (8 inch) round sandwich tins.
2 Place the eggs and caster sugar in a large bowl and whisk with an electric hand beater until the mixture is thick, creamy and leaves a trail on the surface when the whisk is lifted out.
3 Sieve the flour, cocoa powder and baking powder on to the surface of the mixture and then fold in carefully. Add the vanilla extract and the orange zest when the folding is nearly complete.
4 Divide the mixture evenly between the two sandwich tins and put into the oven immediately. Bake for 15–20 minutes until the sponge is golden, risen and set and just beginning to come away from the sides of the tin. Turn the sponges out on to a wire rack to cool.
5 To make the filling, mix together with the Greek yogurt and the marmalade. Reserve the rind. Peel and segment the orange, discarding any pith, chop it roughly and stir into the ricotta mixture. Place one of the sponges on to a serving plate and spread over the filling. Carefully place the other sponge on top.
6 To make the topping, put the plain chocolate and butter into a small bowl and place over a pan of barely simmering water until melted. Drizzle over the cake, allowing the topping to dribble over the edges. Take the rind from the orange and finely slice. Put the caster sugar in a pan with 1 tablespoon water. Heat gently to dissolve, then increase the heat and boil for a few minutes. Add the sliced rind and boil again for a few minutes. Drain and allow to cool. Top the cake decoratively with the rind.
7 Chill the gateau lightly before serving but do not allow to become too cold or the flavour will be lost. Cut into 8 or 12 portions to serve.

CHOCOLATE ORANGE CELEBRATION GATEAU

MAKES 12
PREPARATION & COOKING TIME:
15 minutes + 25 minutes cooking
FREEZING: recommended

PER SERVING: 222 calories, 10 g fat

Muffins make an **ideal breakfast food** or a healthy addition to a lunchbox. Home made muffins are far superior to shop-bought varieties, and using vegetable oil instead of melted butter in this recipe means that saturated fat is avoided. Muffins are best eaten within a couple of days of being made (if you have any left over, that is!). Otherwise, keep them in the freezer and speedily defrost them in the microwave when required.

CRANBERRY, APPLE & OAT MUFFINS

75 g (2³/₄ oz) rolled oats
250 ml (9 fl oz) semi skimmed milk
200 g (7 oz) plain white flour
3 teaspoons baking powder
¹/₄ teaspoon salt
¹/₂ teaspoon ground cinnamon
75 g (2³/₄ oz) dried cranberries
1 crisp eating apple, peeled, cored and diced
75 g (2³/₄ oz) soft light brown sugar
1 egg
100 ml (3¹/₂ fl oz) vegetable oil
1 teaspoon vanilla extract

1 Preheat the oven to Gas Mark 5/electric oven 190°C/fan oven 170°C. Place 12 paper muffin cases in a muffin tin.

2 Combine the oats and the milk in a medium sized bowl and set aside to soak, allowing the oats to soften.

3 Meanwhile, sift the flour, baking powder, salt and ground cinnamon into a large bowl and mix in the dried cranberries, diced apple and brown sugar.

4 Beat the egg, vegetable oil and vanilla extract into the oat and milk mixture then pour into the dry ingredients. Stir quickly until just combined and no dry flour is visible – do not over mix, or the muffins will be tough.

5 Working quickly, fill the muffin cases three quarters full with mixture and then place in the oven for 20–25 minutes until risen, golden and just firm to the touch. Remove from the oven and transfer to a wire rack to cool slightly. They are delicious if served while still warm.

MAKES 8 PORTIONS
PREPARATION & COOKING TIME:
15 minutes + 1 hour rising
+ 30 minutes cooking
FREEZING: recommended

PER SERVING: 254 calories, 9 g fat

I love the texture of seeded breads and this home made one is no exception. It also helps to know that many edible seeds are a **good source of minerals** and polyunsaturated fats.

SEEDED BREAD

200 g (7 oz) strong white flour
200 g (7 oz) strong wholemeal flour
¹/₂–1 teaspoon salt
1 teaspoon sugar
7 g sachet fast action yeast
2 tablespoons sunflower seeds
2 tablespoons sesame seeds
1 tablespoon poppy seeds
2 tablespoons sunflower oil
plus extra for greasing
a little milk to glaze (optional)

1 Place the flours, salt, sugar, dried yeast and seeds in a large mixing bowl and stir to combine. Make a well in the centre of the dry ingredients.
2 Pour in the sunflower oil and 250–300 ml (9–10 fl oz) lukewarm water. Mix together to form a soft dough.
3 Turn the dough out on to a floured work surface and knead for 10 minutes until the dough is smooth and elastic. Divide into eight equal pieces and shape into rolls.
4 Lightly grease a 20 cm (8 inch) round sandwich tin. Place one of the rolls in the centre and arrange the others evenly around the edge. Cover with lightly oiled clingfilm and leave in a warm place for about 1 hour until risen and doubled in size – the rolls should have merged into each other.

5 Preheat the oven to Gas Mark 7/electric oven 220°C/fan oven 200°C.
6 Brush the top of the dough with a little milk if desired. Place in the oven and bake for 10 minutes, then reduce the temperature to Gas Mark 4/electric oven 180°C/fan oven 160°C and bake for a further 15–20 minutes. The bread is cooked when the top is golden brown and the base sounds hollow when tapped. Leave to cool on a wire rack, then tear into portions to serve.

MAKES 2 ROUND LOAVES
PREPARATION & COOKING TIME:
20 minutes + 1 hour rising + 30 minutes cooking
FREEZING: recommended

SUNBLUSH TOMATO & OLIVE BREAD

A brilliant Mediterranean style bread, **ideal for accompanying soups and salads**. Do try to use sunblush tomatoes, instead of sun-dried, since they are more succulent, brighter in colour and look better in the dough. They can generally be bought loose at deli counters.

PER SERVING: 223 calories, 6 g fat

600 g (1 lb 5oz) strong white flour
7 g sachet of fast action yeast
1 teaspoon salt
2 teaspoons dried basil
100 g (3^1/$_2$ oz) stoned black olives, chopped roughly
100 g (3^1/$_2$ oz) sunblush tomatoes, chopped roughly
3 tablespoons extra virgin olive oil
a little vegetable oil for greasing

1   Place the flour, yeast, salt, basil, olives and sunblush tomatoes in a large mixing bowl. Stir together to mix.
2   Make a well in the centre and pour in 375 ml (13 fl oz) of lukewarm water and the olive oil. Stir together to form a soft dough.
3   Turn the dough out on to a floured work surface and knead for 10 minutes until the dough is smooth and elastic.
4   Divide the dough into two equal pieces and shape each piece into a round loaf. Use your fore finger to put dimples in the bread. Place the loaves on two separate lightly greased baking sheets and loosely cover with oiled clingfilm. Leave in a warm place to double in size (about 45–60 minutes).
5   Preheat the oven to Gas Mark 7/electric oven 220°C/fan oven 200°C.
6   Bake the loaves in the oven for 10 minutes, then reduce the temperature to Gas Mark 4/electric oven 180°C/fan oven 160°C and bake for a further 20–25 minutes until the loaves are golden brown and sound hollow when tapped on the base. Leave to cool on a wire rack.

MAKES 18
PREPARATION & COOKING TIME:
10 minutes + 25 minutes cooking
FREEZING: recommended

APRICOT SUNSHINE BARS

This variation on a flapjack is more crumbly in texture than chewy and 100 per cent more **flavour-filled** than the traditional flapjack. Again, the 'heart friendly' fats from the sunflower margarine and the seeds, along with the soluble fibre from the oats, make this a good choice to accompany an afternoon cup of tea or to pop in a lunchbox.

PER SERVING: 173 calories, 11 g fat

150 g (5^1/$_2$ oz) sunflower margarine plus extra for greasing
100 g (3^1/$_2$ oz) golden syrup
50 g (1^3/$_4$ oz) soft light brown sugar
225 g (7 oz) rolled oats
50 g (1^3/$_4$ oz) sunflower seeds
50 g (1^3/$_4$ oz) sesame seeds
100 g (3^1/$_2$ oz) ready to eat dried apricots, chopped

1   Preheat the oven to Gas Mark 4/electric oven 180°C/fan oven 160°C. Lightly grease a 28 x 19 cm (11 x 7^1/$_2$ inch) baking tin with a little sunflower margarine.
2   In a large saucepan, melt together the margarine, golden syrup and brown sugar – do not allow to boil.
3   Stir in the oats, sunflower and sesame seeds and dried apricots. Mix well and then transfer to the baking tin. Spread the mixture evenly in the tin and press down lightly.
4   Bake in the oven for 20–25 minutes until lightly golden. Remove from the oven and leave to cool for 5 minutes, then mark into 18 squares with a knife.
5   When completely cold, cut through the squares, lift them out of the tin and store in an airtight container.

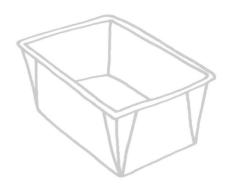